this page is intentionally left blank.

RESULTS MATTER

Six Questions to Make You a Better Leader
(And a Better Person)

An Easy and Proven Leadership Approach with Strategies for Motivating your Team, Tactics to Drive Accountability and Solutions on How to Achieve your Goals.

Joseph P. Connelly

Results Matter: Six Questions to Make You a Better Leader (And a Better Person)

Joseph P. Connelly

No part of this book was created using A.I.
Like flowers and people, artificial doesn't always mean better.

© 2023 by Straight Shooters Marketing

All rights reserved. No part of this book may be reproduced, distributed, or transmitted in any form or by any means, including photocopying, recording or other electronic or mechanical methods, without the prior written permission of Straight Shooters Marketing.

www.resultsmatter.app

For more information, email info@resultsmatter.app.

Cover Design & Layout: Riley Miller, info@skymillz.com

ISBN: 978 0 969 3785-2-5

To my wonderful mother,

Elizabeth Connelly,

who taught me the values of

hard work and integrity.

CONTENTS

Foreword: Early Thoughts about Leadership . . . ix

Introduction: Leadership is Broken xv

PART I – LEADERSHIP FUNDAMENTALS

1. . . . . .Leadership Begins with Balance   1
2. . . . . Leadership Is About Results   9
3. . . . . . The Leadership Tools that Drive Results   17

PART II – CREATE THE PLAN

4. . . . Six Questions to Make You a Better Leader   27
5. . . . . . . Question One – Why Are We Here?   33
6. . Question Two – What Does Success Look Like?   39
7. . . . . Question Three – How Do We Get There?   45
8. . . . . Question Four – Who Does What, When?   51
9. . . . . . .Question Five – How Are You Doing?   57

10.	Question Six – How Are We Doing?	63
11.	Applying the Full Accountability Matrix	69
12.	The Onboarding Accountability Matrix	75

PART III – FOCUS THE TEAM

13.	Introduction to Personality Profiles	87
14.	There Are Only Four Types of People in the World	95
15.	The Drivers	103
16.	The Amiables	111
17.	The Expressives	117
18.	The Thinkers	123

PART IV – BE THE LEADER

19.	Leading The Team	129
20.	Keeping the Trust	139
21.	Final Words	149

Epilogue	155
Appendix: Onboarding Checklist	157
Acknowledgements	159
About the Author	161
Endnotes	163

FOREWORD

Early Thoughts about Leadership

My interest in leadership began at an early age. I can remember when I was about nine years old and my eldest brother was leaving the house to go to college. One of the things he left behind was a brown plaque, which had the following quotation on it, often attributed to Edmund Burke:

> *The only thing necessary*
> *for the triumph of evil*
> *is for good men to do nothing.*[1]

Later in life, I learned that Edmund Burke was born in Dublin, Ireland, in 1729. He attended Trinity College and then went on to London, finding success as a writer, politician, and philosopher. He sat in the House of Commons as a Member of Parliament with the Whig Party and is widely regarded as the founder of modern conservatism.[2]

Much later in life, I was disappointed to discover that Burke never actually said those words.[3] In spite of this misattribution, Burke still had many brilliant quotes, including the famous, "Those that don't know history are doomed to repeat it," but it is the first quote ("The only thing necessary…") which has hung on my wall for about the past fifty years and clearly shaped my early impressions of leaders.

From my youth, my earliest thoughts about leadership were that leaders take action.

> *Leaders are the ones who jump in and correct the wrong. Actions, not words, are the ultimate results of leadership.*[4]
> *–Bill Owens, American politician*

The popular television and comic book heroes of the time supported my early impressions of action leadership. Regardless of whether it was Batman, Superman, or Spiderman, the hero always took action to defeat the bad guy. Even the Royal Canadian Mounted Police always "got their man."

My mother, being an educator and historian, ensured my family knew our history, and specifically one epic British political battle right before World War II. The battle was between Neville Chamberlain, who wanted appeasement with Germany, and his steadfast opponent, Winston Churchill, who wanted to stand up to Hitler. The victory eventually went to Churchill, but it was a dark time, as Hitler quickly overran virtually all of Europe

Interestingly, every source on leadership I found while researching this book almost always included Churchill, and often Hitler, but never mentioned former Prime Minister Neville Chamberlain.[5]

We will always remember Churchill for his famous speech, which galvanized a nation and mobilized every citizen to help in any way possible.

> *We shall go on to the end, we shall fight in France,*
> *we shall fight on the seas and oceans,*
> *we shall fight with growing confidence and growing strength in the air,*
> *we shall defend our Island, whatever the cost may be,*
> *we shall fight on the beaches, we shall fight on the landing grounds,*
> *we shall fight in the fields and in the streets, we shall fight in the hills;*
> *we shall never surrender.*[6]

Over eighty years later, his speech is still recognized as one of the greatest calls to action in human history, and my mother quoted it often.

Real-life leaders of my era included the likes of John F. Kennedy, John Lennon, and Martin Luther King. They were always in the news. They gave speeches, held marches, and Lennon even protested in bed. They were always doing something: something positive, something good. They were always taking action.

Thus, to me, leaders were good men (and women) who stepped in to do what was right.

My strict Catholic upbringing reinforced this leadership concept of taking action and doing the right thing.

> ***Action is the foundational key to all success.*** [7]
> *–Pablo Picasso*

Its was the late 1960s and there was considerable social turmoil. At the time, the United States had a lot of challenges with divisive wars, wide-ranging drafts, and ongoing nationwide protests. Like today, there were many opposing views.

In the early 1970s, this turmoil appeared in Canada with internal terrorists called the Front de libération du Québec (FLQ) and the imposition of the War Measures Act.

In addition, substantial rifts appeared in society between the old and young, left and right, and even, dare I say it, suits and hippies (to use those terms of the day). The battle was real for both sides, with each side depicting the other as the evil one.

Fast forward to today and see that these divisions still exist and have only become more acute on all sides. In a world where we need to work together more closely than ever before, the battle lines are drawn between left and right, east and west, urban and rural, and in many instances, the voters and government (the constant protests at every level of government are a clear demonstration of this). This division has created unparalleled animosity and an atmosphere of mistrust and suspicion seemingly everywhere. Working together is more difficult than ever.

Here is an interesting test. Ask your peers to name a great leader of today. I have done this many times, and people struggle to produce a single name; even if you do, others will often challenge you for your choice.

In this atmosphere of polarization, often two parties who must collaborate have difficulty just sitting at the same table. Even once the various parties get to the table, zero trust virtually guarantees zero results. How do we get these divergent parties on the same page?

Results do matter, but work environments today are very fluid and temporary, so results are more elusive than ever before. Innovative approaches must be flexible and simple. This book creates a leadership process using six questions to bring people together and focus their efforts, thereby creating greater results.

I am fortunate to have worked for legendary billionaires, maverick entrepreneurs, blue-chip organizations, encouraging start-ups, and even a few not-for-profit organizations, and this experience has allowed me to study many strong leaders. One common theme with these leaders is that they deliver. They know how to get things done and produce results. Leaders can't really be leaders unless they produce results.

Sadly, I have also seen some poor examples of leadership and too many of what Canadian psychologist Jordan Peterson would describe as "individuals unencumbered with those pedestrian traits of personality and common sense."

Just as there are good and poor doctors and lawyers, there are good leaders and poor leaders. We need to recognize what works for good leadership and dissolve what isn't working. Sadly, as I will outline, a lot is not working in leadership development.

I began this leadership journey by studying many of the ancient and modern thoughts about leadership. I examined the major challenges and specifically asked leaders about their road to success, as well as their roadblocks. Many of those roadblocks involved personality conflicts or people management. For that reason, there is considerable material generated in this book to assist leaders in understanding themselves, their teams, and what motivates the individuals within the team.

Most of my career was in project management of some type, so this book is my small part in trying to create a process to help move a project forward. Frequently throughout my career, I have been asked to recover a project from the brink of collapse, and I utilized much of the material presented in this book to do just that.

The process I have developed is focused on six critical questions that provide clarity at every step in the project, so everyone agrees right from the start. The answers to the questions form the core of an accountability matrix, which serves to monitor the project until the goals are achieved.

Once I fully developed the concept, I took it to the business and educational community. The feedback from both was very encouraging, so I formally developed a supporting app (resultsmatter.app) and this accompanying book.

INTRODUCTION

Leadership Is Broken

Losers have goals, winners have systems.[8]
–Scott Adams, American cartoonist and writer

I have noticed that many leaders of today, especially politicians, have far too many goals and too few systems on how to achieve those goals.

When you write a book, you typically begin by doing research on the subject. In my case, I wanted to author a book on leadership, so naturally I researched leadership, leadership theories, and examples of good and bad leadership. When we think of leaders, we often think about our political leaders. Today, the only thing lower than the leadership landscape is the political landscape.

Please allow me to begin with a sampling of quotations to support this contention from the left, the right, and academia.

> *We need leadership which brings our people together and makes us stronger.*[9]
> *–Bernie Sanders, American politician*

> *In the 2020s, however, in our supposedly advanced democracies, the political leitmotif has been one of feeble and failing leadership.*[10]
> *–Freddy Gray, Deputy Editor, The Spectator*

> *We don't know why or how such an unimpressive cadre ended up running the government, only that they are here and the American people are suffering from their presence.*[11]
> *-Victor Davis Hanson, Professor Emeritus, California State University*

Even the economist Martin Armstrong has little positive to add:

We have the most incompetent crop of world leaders perhaps in human history.

I think it would be fair to say, regardless of people's politics, that we have a leadership problem in society today.

Social psychologist Jonathan Haidt asks, "Why has the past 10 years of American life has been uniquely stupid?" He argues that the best way to understand the chaos and fragmentation of American society is to see ourselves as the citizens of Babel in the days after God rendered them unable to understand one another.

It is so easy to source quotes about the poor state of leadership today—I could literally fill a book. When the meme of the year is a picture from the Mediterranean of a donkey leading a herd of sheep on a country road, it speaks volumes about leadership. I find it ironic that the effects of poor leadership are even being seen in—you guessed it—leadership schools.

A recent *Harvard Business Review* report entitled "Educating the Next Generation of Leaders" (*Harvard Business Review*, Mar. 2019) identified three large gaps in leadership development.

1. Long-term motivations of the company are inconsistent with the short-term intentions of the employee
2. Lack of interpersonal skills, particularly how to communicate and work efficiently
3. Weak skills transfer between the classroom and the office

As the saying goes, leadership teachers and trainers have but one job to do and they don't seem to be getting it done.

For a long time, I have felt that a lot of the efforts with leadership training centred on developing better attributes for the leader. My research on leadership programs indicates many instructors support this idea of molding the leader. Somewhere along the way, leadership training became attributes training. We became confused with what leadership really is; so much so, we now seem to celebrate the most basic of accomplishments while fawning over mediocre attributes. There is barely a mention of any actual results these days, and I fear the methods for achieving results may become a mystery for an entire generation.

Further, consider that every year, thousands of leadership books and training seminars are released, but we still seem to be missing the mark.

As a society, we should be getting better at leadership, yet we all are suffering through significant and questionable decisions that often include a host of unintended consequences and unknown harms.

Besides this declining quality of leadership and dwindling number of good leaders, there appears to be a "dumbing down" of the general population.

The American College Test (ACT) is a standard test used for college admission. In 2022, over 1.5 million US students took the test, and the results can only be described as dismal. This year, ACT reported the lowest average scores in thirty-one years. Subjects including science, math, reading, English, and composite scores have been dropping rapidly since 2016.[12]

For over 50 years, the University of Chicago has tracked a measurable decline in IQ scores across three major groups. Since the 1960's, high school graduates' IQs have dropped by 6%, college graduates by 13%, and graduate students by 8%.[13]

Sadly, we see not only many people with lower IQs, but also a lot fewer people with higher IQs.[14] The issue may be compounded by the Dunning-Kruger effect, where people with minimal talent and experience overstate their abilities, thereby, getting in way over their heads. The Peter Principle, where individuals rise in an organization one or two levels higher than their abilities justify, happens in today's business world with confounding regularity.

I have observed throughout my career many individuals who desire the traditional business titles of leadership, yet do not know how to motivate people nor have a clue on how to achieve results.

Why is it we cannot seem to teach leadership?

Why is it the quality of our leadership in just about every arena possible appears to be getting worse?

One of my favourite quotations is "discontent is the first necessity of all progress" by Thomas Edison. If we are all content and satiated, we would have no desire to change anything, and nothing would get done. Discontent is the motivation for change and improvement, and let's just say, I harbour considerable discontent over the state of our leadership.

My research has indicated that where there is poor leadership, problems quickly surface, whether in the boardroom or the classroom. Unfair or uneven workloads, lack of accountability, murky goals, and poor follow-up are often cited as symptoms of poor leadership in both arenas.

The 2019 Harvard Business Review study makes me wonder if we can even teach leadership, but I know that if we focus on results, we can certainly achieve better results.

This book presents a demonstrated method to achieve better results.

> *Throw away those books on inspirational leadership, send the consultants packing! Know your job, set a good example for the people under you and put results over politics.*[15]
> –Dylan Machan, contributing editor, *Forbes* and *Wall Street Journal*

I wrote about the turbulent 1960s in the foreword, but today we are even more divided.

Polarized opinions are clear in politics, energy, economics, education, food, health, religion, and even gender. It is difficult to name anything we do agree on. With all of these challenges so very evident, where are the leaders with the solutions? Where is the plan to move beyond this impasse? Rome burns while Nero plays a tune.

We need to get back to basics and start thinking about roadmaps for how to drive actual results. We need processes that bring ideas and quality plans that enhance our understanding. We need better leaders to champion all of this.

If we want better leaders, we need to show leaders, and teams for that matter, a way to achieve results. We begin by examining the three key elements of any project: creating the plans, focusing the team, and being the leader.

Figure 1. Key Elements of Any Project

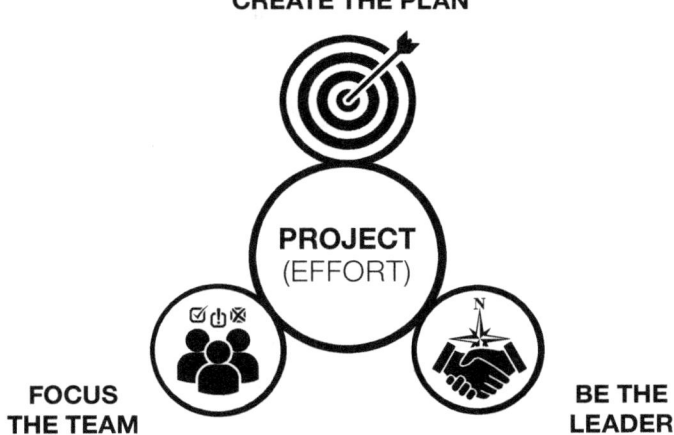

Create the plan: Every successful project has a plan to get to success. The answers to the six questions provided will generate an accountability matrix to manage the project and for the team to follow and deliver on.

Focus the team: Following the creation of the plan, the book continues with an examination of the most important asset of any project, the people on that project. The goal here is to focus the team by understanding the team members' individual motivations. While I can identify that there are only four types of people in the world, I know that doesn't make getting them focussed any easier. However, great leaders know their team's personalities so well, they can accurately predict individuals' behaviours and team interactions.

Be the leader: Near the end of the book, you get to be the leader by reviewing typical interpersonal challenges around communication, time management, and decision making. Conflict, the loss of trust, and how to build it back closes out the leadership section.

Results Matter: Six Questions to Make You a Better Leader was developed because I, like many others, was not satisfied with the state of leadership. As Scott Adams said, "Winners have systems," so when I couldn't find a system to drive results, I created my own, which I present here in six questions.

I sincerely hope you find value in every chapter and solid results in every effort.

PART 1

Leadership Fundamentals

*If you have knowledge,
let others light their candles in it.*
–Margaret Fuller, Woman in the Nineteenth Century, 1843

CHAPTER 1

Leadership Begins with Balance

If you are fortunate enough to have been to New York City, you know that one of the major attractions is the Statue of Liberty. She is a stunning sight as she rises over three hundred feet above Liberty Island to welcome tourists, immigrants, and returning Americans. France gave the Statue of Liberty to the United States to celebrate America's first one hundred years as a nation. Her design is based on Libertas, the Roman goddess of freedom, and a similar statue graces the dome of the US capital in Washington, D.C.

Originally called La Liberte Eclairant le Monde (Liberty Enlightening the World), the statue is full of symbolism, from the broken shackles at her feet representing the overthrow of tyranny and oppression to her seven-spike crown for both the seven continents and seven seas.

We see her as moving, stepping forward to a better future and leading the way to enlightenment, showing all the path to freedom.

If you look deeper, you will find much more symbolism.

In her right hand, she holds the torch, held high to enlighten the world to the value of liberty. At the time the statute was erected, the French described this light as "not the torch that sets afire," but what is called the flambeau, the candle-flame that "enlightens" (think reading by candlelight).[16]

Her torch is symbolic of the knowledge and intelligence that brings new enlightenment to the people. The emergence of the rational individual is a key part of this new world.

In the statue's left hand is a tabula ansata (a tablet with handles), representing a tablet of laws. The tablet is inscribed with the date of the creation of the United States, July IV, MDCCLXXVI (July 4, 1776) with the signing of the Declaration of Independence.[17]

The shape of the tablet is that of a keystone, an architectural stone that is critical because it keeps all the other pieces together. The tablet recognizes a society based on law because "without law, freedom and democracy would not prevail."[18]

These contrasting symbols, held in the Statue of Liberty's hands, provide an interesting dichotomy that shows the key challenge for all leaders.

In her left hand, there are always rules or norms, such as those provided in the tablet's symbolism. This is the authority side of leadership.

In her right hand, there is enlightenment and the influence or reason approach to leadership.

We often understand leadership to begin with this delicate balance between these two approaches, between push and pull, between authority and reason.

> *Fortune indeed is the man who takes*
> *exactly the right measure of himself.*[19]
> *–Peter Mere Latham, English physician*

An authority-based model of leadership includes a command-and-control approach to managing the group. Compliance through rules and regulations is clear and most activities are process-driven. Team behaviours are managed through direct discipline and often enforced with the threat of consequences. These types of teams usually have severe time constraints, so no options are available for debate or reaching consensus. Such would be the case in the event of a military operation or emergency services.

> *If my house is on fire, the last thing I want
> is a focus group of firefighters discussing
> the best way to put it out.*[20]
> *–Joseph P. Connelly, Results Matter seminar*

The other end of the scale from the command-and-control model is the influence or reason model. Here, the leader has the time and character to gain personal commitments from each team member. That in turn drives behaviours toward a common goal or value. Behaviours are "supercharged" through inspiration, trust, and solid relationships. This team is free thinking and can and will break the rules in their quest for a solution. This does not happen with the authoritarian approach. The influential leader establishes relationships between teammates to encourage creativity. Everyone genuinely likes each other (most of the time) and is committed to not letting the others down. Individual coaching motivates both teams and leaders to model the key behaviours sought. Loyalty to the organization and the project is clear.

> *There is a difference between
> giving directions and giving direction.*[21]
> *–Simon Sinek, author*

These two leadership approaches exist on a push-pull continuum. There are times to push the team just a little and sometimes quite a bit (to make a deadline or budget). There can also be other circumstances that require a different approach. In those cases, the leader may pull the team along (with reason to enlightenment and new knowledge). [22]

A good leader knows under what circumstances to employ what method.

In this book, we will look at leadership at the extremes to fully understand the underlying behaviours and motivations of both leaders and people in general. It is easier to identify behaviours at the extremes because they are so obvious. Few people are one hundred per cent one way or another; rather, a rich blend between the two extremes.

A good example to show the differences in these two approaches is how each type would react to new challenges.

The authoritarian approach to challenges would begin by overstating or overestimating the impact of the challenge (of course, with the required wringing of hands and gnashing of teeth, as authoritarians generally do not like change or challenges). Every possible negative consequence, regardless of the dim possibility of it occurring, would be well evaluated. The solutions could even include a "no solution" by avoiding the challenge entirely (the "Well then—let's just not do anything" attitude).

This core value of risk avoidance for the authoritarian creates an urgency, so solutions are often quickly developed, secretive, and short term in nature. As a result, the solution can often address only the symptoms and not change the challenge (i.e., the original problem may remain or return soon).

Meanwhile, the reason approach is more long term and looks at challenges as opportunities to be carefully studied. The leader presents the challenge to many individuals to gain insight into others' ideas and to develop creative solutions. The challenge is treated like a team-building opportunity. In these cases, you can see how this solution may involve more risk, yet often includes the possibility of more reward. Ironically, the risk involved can sometimes be downplayed or even dismissed under this reason approach.

Figure 2. Leadership Begins with Balance

(*Dominates*) Authority	Reason (*Motivates*)
Pushes	Pulls
Focuses on details	Focuses on direction
Instructs	Encourages
Eyes bottom line	Eyes potential
Approves	Motivates
Dominates	Delegates
Has objectives	Has vision
Is all about control	Is all about trust

A straightforward way to remember these two approaches is that authority tells (dominates) while reason sells (motivates), and we have all worked, more or less, for one of these types. Fortunately, few people are one hundred per cent one way or another, and there are obvious applications where one approach is better than another. Leadership begins with balance, and good leaders know when to push and when to pull.

It is, however, important to recognize these two approaches because when they are employed in the wrong environments, chaos ensues. If we are truly trying to create more leaders, we must begin by acknowledging that these two approaches have their place, both with drawbacks and advantages.

To successfully lead, you first need to know yourself as a leader, the group you lead, the interactions within this group, and the interactions between this group and others.

Whether your leadership approach is leaning toward authority or reason, you can see how your balance between the two approaches would affect all your team interactions. Here I raise the mirror for you to examine your own leadership approach (more push or more pull) and realize the effect of your leadership style on the team. As renowned automaker Lee Iacocca once observed, "the speed of the boss is the speed of the team".

Leadership begins with balance, but it certainly doesn't end there. Both the reason and authority approaches provide a foundational base from which to grow your knowledge of leadership.

I think legendary management expert Peter Drucker probably said it best.

> *Your first and foremost job as a leader is*
> *to take charge of your own energy and then*
> *help orchestrate the energy of those around them.*[23]

Notice how the quote begins with the leader's own energy. All leaders have energy that is displayed in how they manage their people. For example, and at the most basic level, is the general leadership approach one of push or pull? The team will, in turn, develop a collective energy that is dictated by the personality preference of the leader.

Therefore, as a leader, you need to know what form your energy takes with your people. This is very important because leadership of people is often a "situational art" and an authoritarian approach does not always work with people. Similarly, the reason approach doesn't always work because some people just prefer to be told what to do.

Regardless of whether your approach is one of authority or reason, your own energy will be reflected in your team. Your energy can be overt or subtle, but it must be there in some form to motivate others.

You also need to know the team's energy and how to help orchestrate or direct it. That means you need to know about your team. Your team needs to know you care about them. Your people need to know that you give a damn. As a leader, if you don't care about the people, the project, or the company, why should your team care?

> *A different world can never be built*
> *with indifferent people.*[24]
> *–E.W. Palmer, Rotarian*

KEY LESSON

As the leader, you are primarily responsible for results. As shown in this chapter, leadership begins with a balance between an authority approach (push) and a reason approach (pull). They exist on a continuum, with each approach having benefits and drawbacks, and their application is usually dictated by that situation, the individuals involved, and the time constraints identified.

CHAPTER 2

*There are two types of people.
People who accomplish things and
people who claim to have accomplished things.
The first group is less crowded.
–Mark Twain*

CHAPTER 2

Leadership Is about Results

To be a leader, one must have won a battle, an election, a debate, a contest, or gained a notable degree of public recognition. I often say leaders have usually won something specific, something special, and/or something large. Leaders can come from any kind of background and excel in many fields, such as the military, business, arts, religion, politics, or sports.

To be clear—a leader has gained or achieved a result.

Every year, it is my honour to speak to university students, usually in their third year. In the early presentations, I regaled them with stories from the business world, politics, or tourism.

After a few years, I began to feel that, while being very entertaining, I needed to provide the students with something more useful. I approached their professor and requested the opportunity to move the discussion toward leadership. At the very beginning, I remember not being sure what exactly I was looking for, but I hoped to develop something of value, a tool to help them get better results within a team environment.

> *A great change leader creates other change leaders.*[25]
> *–Dr. John Kotter, Harvard professor*

I always opened the class with the same provocative question: what makes a great leader?

"Look around," I said. "Look at the person next to you. Are they a leader? Are you? All of you, whether you believe it or not, are the leaders of tomorrow. You are at one of the best universities in the country, in one of the best countries in the world. While not an absolute rule, the fact remains, most of the leaders of today are university educated. So you, my friends, are it."

I then cycle back and asked them, "So if you are all the leaders of tomorrow, I ask again, what makes a great leader?"

They slowly begin to offer up answers. I carefully recorded their responses, and soon the whiteboard was filled with forty or more different statements, such as, be trustworthy, lead with respect, be decisive, and be a team player. Many of the suggestions, like these last two, could be considered opposites.

The interesting thing about these answers is that while each of these attributes would be considered a worthy addition to any character, they do not necessarily guarantee success (i.e., they do not guarantee results). As I like to say, "Just because you may be tall, that doesn't mean you can play basketball."

Certainly, many of these attributes identified could be included in the previously outlined reasoned approach, and those "softer" attributes ultimately mean a more harmonic workplace. We all desire a workplace free of stress with "easy" superiors, but that doesn't stretch the team's abilities nor allow for individual growth. Again, the aforementioned balance comes into play. There are ideal times to push and times to pull.

While employees appreciate the enlightened approach and the easygoing management style that comes with it, a consequence can be a negative impact on the potential results.

As I continued my research, I examined the current business thoughts on the question of what makes a great leader. I reviewed significant blue-chip material from some well-known business names like Entrepreneur, Forbes, Fast Company, Fortune, Indeed, Inc., and LinkedIn. Surely these brand names could provide some background and direction on my question of what makes a great leader.

With articles such as "Seven Keys to Becoming a Remarkably Effective Leader" (Inc., 2016.)[26], "Four Keys to Great Leadership" (Forbes, 2012)[27], and "Three Keys to Influential Leadership" (Fast Company, 2015)[28], I began to think there was an overabundance of keys to leadership and the real key was to have less keys.

Again, as with the university students, there were far too many keys (or attributes) for any leader to track, much less follow. These keys were often unique (i.e., no repeats) and produced another laundry list of desirable personality attributes. Here is a sample of some of those attributes.

Figure 3. What Makes a Great Leader?

Have vision	Be focused
Provide motivation	Communicate
Display passion	Secure relationships
Be decisive	Be honest
Be persuasive	Care
Be a team builder	Inspire commitment
Have character	Reveal your true self
Maintain strategic control	Face challenges
Seek feedback	Be transparent
Win trust	Find balance
Empower people	Be authentic
Maintain values	Put others' needs above your own
Earn respect	Give up the need to be liked
Delegate wisely	Stay curious
Be resilient	Set goals
Give employees time	Reward achievement
Do not take it too seriously	Think long-term solutions

(My favourite of these attributes is the obvious, give up the need to be liked. If you hold any delusions about your own need to be liked, being a leader is probably not for you. No one goes into leadership to be liked. Leadership is not about being liked, but rather, about helping others become more successful).

Leadership is definitely not about changing your personality type to fit some leadership ideal. I will expand on this idea later in the Focus the Team section but my mother would always say, "People don't change". Attempting to change an attribute has a lifespan of about three to six weeks. The leopard can't change its spots and people cannot magically change their personality.

For example, I don't know if you could have ever told Steve Jobs to be nicer to the good folks in HR, or give personality advice to Barack Obama or Donald Trump, or any results-focused leader of our time.

I returned to the post-secondary students with the very long list of attributes, and we chatted more about them and how the attributes applied to leadership.

At this point, I introduced them to another famous quote by management expert Peter Drucker (and the main premise of this book).

> *Effective leadership is not about making speeches or being liked.*
> *Leadership is defined by results, not attributes.*[29]

In the end, the students agreed that a system whereby leaders could improve their results was needed (i.e., essentially - better at getting better results). They were most interested in a system that could help them with their term-long, team project.

The students were quite candid in relating to me their frustrations with their term-long, team projects where accountability and uneven workload were constant issues. Further, they lacked a consistent model or framework from which to work for team projects. They wanted something that brought everyone onto one page or at least one common expectation.

Interestingly, I heard these same complaints about accountability and workload in the business community as well. That was encouraging, as

I believed I could develop a simple approach to results that would work in both schools and businesses.

> *A leader's singular job is to get results.*[30]
> *–Harvard Business Review, 2000*

KEY LESSON

Great leadership is about achieving quality results.

Quality results are determined by the quality of the plan, the personalities of the team members, and the approach of the leader.

Leadership is not about your creativity nor your popularity. It is not about how nice you are nor how smart you are. Leadership is not about your attributes nor how well you delegate.

Leadership is about results. Period.

CHAPTER 3

Talk doesn't cook rice.
–Chinese proverb

CHAPTER 3

The Leadership Tools that Drive Results

The time has never been more pressing for a results-based leadership model because, despite all the education, personal development, and leadership coaching, we still seem to be failing when it comes to teaching leadership.

> *More than 50% of senior leaders believe that their talent development efforts do not adequately build critical skills or organizational capabilities.*[31]
> *–Harvard Business Review, 2019*

Further, the same study reveals that "anecdotal evidence on skills transfer suggest that only 10% of the $200 billion annual outlay for corporate training and development in the United States delivers concrete results."[32]

To be clear, that is a $180 billion-dollar mistake occurring every year.

There are many other studies that support this sad reality, but our job is not to criticize the efforts of the past, but rather to create some new plans that will assist in better results for better leaders.

Order unchecked will quickly descend into chaos. That is the basis of entropy, where uncertainty and disorder can creep in. Any management process that can help create order would have to be deemed valuable.

Further, similar to the aforementioned attributes list I generated, technology has created many more inputs than any human can even grasp, never mind manage. Today's IT can measure virtually anything, but the key is to measure the right things and not be distracted or misled by non-productive measurements.

With that in mind, I hoped to create a system that could manage many of the inputs required by any leader. The challenge of many inputs, changing variables, and unique personalities creates many demands and opens the possibility for different outcomes (some undesirable). I envisioned a effective system to help keep the order, manage changes, and measure the right things.

> *We know that leadership is very much related to change. As the pace of change accelerates, there is naturally a greater need for effective leadership.*[33]
> *–Dr. John Kotter, Harvard professor*

To truly create better leaders, we should begin by examining all the management functions or roles required. We will begin with an examination the five functions of management, as provided by Koontz and O'Donnell.[34]

Planning

Organizing

Controlling

Staffing

Directing

I like to break the function of directing down further, based on the target audience involved with that communication. In my model, directing is broken down into communicating externally and communicating internally.

Let's examine each of these functions individually, as they will show you how the six questions to make you a better leader were originally generated.

Planning

A leader must set the mission, creating an action-based statement articulating the purpose of the organization.

Organizing

Once the mission is set, a vision needs to be documented about what you hope to accomplish when you execute that mission.

Controlling

As the leader responsible for results, you need plans and processes in place to realize the payoff, including resources utilization and performance measures for the organization.

Staffing

Now that the plan and the processes are clear, is time to assign the people to the critical roles of who does what. Ensuring the right people are in the right roles, more than anything else, dictates the speed and success of a project.

Communicating Internally

Communicating internally usually involves identifying significant internal changes, challenges, or performance updates for the staff, your peers, or your immediate supervisors.

Communicating Externally

Communicating externally is normally defined as messaging being external to the company. Communicating externally is typically about achieving organizational milestones and promoting progress on corporate goals.

If the six roles outlined above are developed correctly and executed efficiently, the overall effort will drive results.

To complicate matters further, however, those roles outlined above also have to apply to many different individual departments, such as marketing, accounting, sales, HR, legal, IT, and customer service. How does a leader tie all these different departments together under one vision, solidly united and suitably motivated?

22   THE LEADERSHIP TOOLS THAT DRIVE RESULTS

As my Canadian friends in tourism would say, How do we get everyone in the same canoe and paddling in the same direction?

> *A genuine leader is not a searcher for consensus, but a molder of consensus.*[35]
> –Martin Luther King Jr.

In the early days of creating the Results Matter approach, I envisioned a prism and how it takes white light and bends it into a rainbow of various colours.

If you could put everything about a prism in reverse and develop a system that would take all those different colours (or functions) and put them through a prism (the system), you could then come out with a common vision at the end (hopefully, all paddling in the same direction).

Figure 4. Management Variables

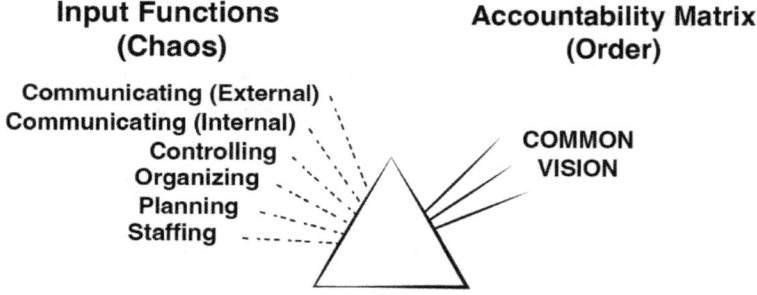

As previously noted, I have benefited from a significant amount of personal development training, in particular, Total Quality Management (TQM). Although the training was several years ago, I can still remember being troubled by the order of some steps. TQM provides a system for management improvements with steps that progress through purpose, process, and payoff, but I was always challenged by how you could put a process ahead of the payoff.

How do you create a path to a target before you clearly define the target?

In my personal management approach, I used purpose, payoff, and then process for my projects, and this seemed better accepted by my team and just made sense. Logically, you first need a payoff from which you can then create a path to that target (process). If your team holds a different vision of what the payoff is, you will end up with several processes to a number of different targets. Clearly identify each payoff first, then work with the team for the best path to that payoff.

Now that the six management roles are identified, we can assign the appropriate leadership tool for each. I have called them the Six P's as the all begin with the letter "P".

For example, under planning, a clear mission or purpose is invaluable in orchestrating the energy of the team toward it. A purpose unites the team and, as we shall see, drives results.

To organize, you need to have a clear payoff to aim for, and that begins with a clear target. With this role, you are organizing everyone around a vision.

Controlling is the execution of the process and the management of the resources. For every payoff there will be a process to get there. Different processes will involve different resources.

While controlling is about all the non-human resource allocation, staffing is about managing human resources and assigning responsibilities. This is often known as the people module.

Internal communication is typically very detailed and involves the evaluation of the individual efforts. This could take the form of an individual performance review; however, it could also be a performance review for a department, division, or even an entire company.

External communication usually involves relating the progress of the team's efforts to the general broad-based payoffs. It is usually any communication beyond the company.

The end results would look like this:

Figure 5. The Six P's

Management Roles	Leadership Tools (Six P's)
Planning	Purpose (*Define the purpose*)
Organizing	Payoff (*Identify the payoff*)
Controlling	Process (*Create the process*)
Staffing	People (*Assign the people*)
Communicating (*Internal*)	Performance (*Review performances*)
Communicating (*External*)	Progress (*Monitor progress*)

The six P's (Purpose, Payoff, Process, People, Performance and Progress) all work together to form the basis of the accountability matrix. We will investigate this matrix in much more detail in subsequent lessons, but I wanted to establish early the connection between the typical management roles and the leadership tools associated with each.

There is a genuine need for a results-based leadership model, which is rooted in our dismal record of creating leaders, as identified by the aforementioned Harvard Business Review study. In fact, our record of just having "committed employees" is in itself a colossal failure (figure 6).

A 2013 Gallop study on the State of the American Workplace[36] found only thirty per cent of those Americans surveyed would describe themselves as committed. Fifty per cent were "putting in time," and twenty per cent would be described as "counterproductive." The report recorded the most frequent cause of this behaviour as "poor leadership." Of course, this study was pre-COVID, but I highly doubt the numbers have improved since that time.

Figure 6. The State of the American Workplace

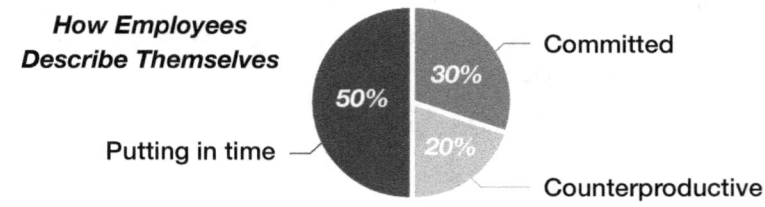

In other research, the value of highly belonging was linked to a fifty-six per cent increase in job performance, yet forty per cent of employees say they feel isolated at work.[37] This underlines the critical importance of engaging or focusing the team, which we examine beginning in chapter 13.

Couple both these findings with a 2013 Harvard study, where they found a correlation between engagement and effectiveness, and we begin to see how Results Matter can only help with the participation and engagement of staff.[38]

KEY LESSON

There are six invaluable tools that every leader needs to fully utilize to drive results. These are referred to as the Six P's and are summarized below.

Leadership Tools (Six P's)

Purpose	Define the purpose of the team, whether a group, department, division or company
Payoff	Identify the payoff of the effort
Process	Create all the processes to deliver the results identified in payoff
People	Assign individuals to specific roles to deliver results
Performance	Regularly review individual performances to track results
Progress	Monitor progress on overall team goals

In the following chapters, each of these tools will be crafted as a series of six questions to assist in completing the accountability matrix.

PART 2

Create The Plan

*The wise man doesn't give the right answers,
he poses the right questions.
–Claude Levi Strauss, Tristes Tropiques
(The Sadness of the Tropics)*

CHAPTER 4

Six Questions to Make You a Better Leader

The first four tools for results are now purpose, payoff, process, and people. Originally, it seemed very natural to have a horizontal orientation, and I actually used this four-part system for some early projects.

With these four tools lined up, they became the core of the model and seemed intuitive.

However, I discovered by stacking these four tools, the first two over the second two, it opened the opportunity to add two more boxes on the end of each row as feedback tools.

If I add two feedback boxes on the end, you end up with a three (horizontal) by two (vertical) matrix with six boxes inside.

Figure 7. The Accountability Matrix

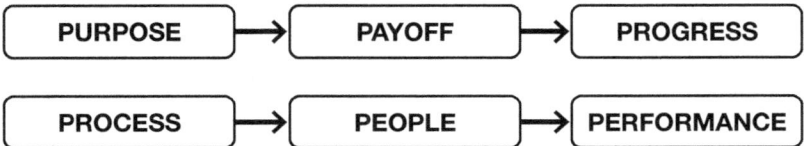

The top row of three boxes deals with corporate activities. The purpose is tied to the payoff of the overall or corporate goals and will be tracked by the progress module.

I managed the individual project activities with the bottom three boxes, identifying the process required, the people involved, and the tracking of the individual performances.

Next, I converted each of these tools to a question to develop the accountability matrix. Hopefully, questions will force teams to think more fully and creatively about the answers. You can add additional questions to draw out better ideas with team members, but these are the key six.

Figure 8. Six Key Questions

Leadership Roles	Leadership Tools	Key Questions
Planning	Purpose	Why are we here?
Organizing	Payoff	What does success look like?
Controlling	Process	How do we get there?
Staffing	People	Who does what, when?
Communicating (int.)	Performance	How are you doing?
Communicating (ext.)	Progress	How are we doing?

This is how I arrived at six simple questions to drive better results. Putting the questions into the matrix creates the following.

Figure 9. Six Questions to Make You a Better Leader

PURPOSE	**PAYOFF**	**PROGRESS**
Why are we here?	What does success look like?	How are we doing?
PROCESS	**PEOPLE**	**PERFORMANCE**
How do we get there?	Who does what, when?	How are you doing?

PART 2

The shadow arrows show the order that the questions should be asked (notice that performance proceeds progress).

Once the answers are provided, they become the input into the accountability matrix. Once the matrix is filled, it serves as the main reference tool to follow the project's progress.

KEY LESSON

In this chapter, we introduced the concept of utilizing six questions to generate the details required for the accountability matrix. The matrix then becomes the key document that manages the project.

CHAPTER 5

*A person who has a why to live for,
can bear any how.
–Friedrich Nietzsche*

CHAPTER 5

The Purpose Question
Why Are We Here?

How many times have you been sitting in a meeting and had to ask yourself, why am I here?

That question could apply to several things, like the meeting you are currently in or the company you currently work for. You could be daydreaming and the "why" may be what gets you out of bed in the morning. I don't want to get too esoteric about an individual's personal purpose on earth, so let's get back to that meeting.

How did you feel when you asked yourself, why am I here?

Disengaged, a bit confused, and maybe even unsure?

Remember that feeling because that is how your team feels if you, as leader, cannot nail the "why" question.

> *A man should look for what is,*
> *and not for what he thinks should be.*[39]
> *–Albert Einstein*

The first step of any project should be to answer as a team, why are we here?

You want to answer that question to identify the purpose, and I find it best answered in a brainstorming exercise. Ask the team to think about it and commit to an answer before discussing. In these cases, it is best to get written answers because it forces some deeper thought and commitment to an answer.

Ask similar questions, such as, Why are we assembled?

What is it we are trying to solve?

What are our team's objectives?

What is our prime directive?

What problem are we trying to solve today?

The questions could be at the company level.

What is our company's mission? Why does this company exist?

You can get even deeper with questions such as, do we live the corporate values or do we just passively embrace them?

Do we connect what we do with what we believe?

Take all your team's thoughts and record them for everyone to see on a whiteboard.

Now ask the team for their original answers and notice how close they were to the group's collective thoughts. How many have changed their "why" after discussing with the team?

This will reveal how closely aligned your team is, but the goal is to ensure thorough discussion and to gain consensus on a common answer that everyone agrees on. Use the white board and provide the exact words.

> *Without a gleaning of purpose in life,
> we have no vision; we live in strife.*[40]
> *–Dean Koontz, author*

This process is a bit of a narrowing exercise, but continually asking "why we are here" sharply defines the project and keeps everyone on the same page right from the beginning.

This question is also a dangerous one.

PART 2

I can remember being in a certain job review and was told that I wasn't taking my current role seriously enough. After a brief moment of thinking about the question, Why am I here? I replied, "You are right, this is not the right place for me," and I quit instantly.

The answer to the question why? can be dangerous in other ways. The answer is critical because it acts as a compass, setting the direction for the effort; however, like a compass, even a small mistake at the start will be amplified on the journey with devastating results. Take your time in agreeing on an answer about why you are here.

> *People do not buy what you do,*
> *they buy why you do it.*[41]
> *–Simon Sinek, author*

The brilliant author Simon Sinek has done considerable research on this subject, and more information can be found in his seminal book, Start with Why. I greatly encourage you to examine his work for a deeper understanding of the why.

This idea of uncovering the why is important because, as Sinek discovered, if we understand why, it moves behaviours and enhances loyalty. For many people, they are what they do. Their job, their position, or their role becomes a big part of who they are. By identifying the purpose, the team member aligns their personal why with the company's why. Having a clear purpose also contributes to the happiness of the individual.

> *You have a sense of our purpose when*
> *you make a valuable contribution to others or to a*
> *society that you find personally meaningful.*[42]
> *–Morten Hansen, professor and author*

It is critical for the entire team to be clear about the right why from the beginning. Remember, the goal is to drive results, and if just one team member is disengaged (wrong motivation), confused (wrong message), or unsure (wrong authority), the results will suffer.

CREATE THE PLAN

Establishing the why with your team is also an excellent opportunity to engage in identifying any recent market developments, or even possible threats early.

Finally, the exercise of asking why with the team allows for another reflection and reinforcement of the organization's core values and their alignment with everyday behaviours and decisions. Memories are mighty short and discussing values and reinforcing them is never a waste of time.

> *Leadership is about three-fourths show the why and one fourth follow up.*[43]
> *–James E. Faust, American religious leader*

KEY LESSON

The answer to the question, why are we here? creates a clear purpose or mission statement that articulates the reason for the effort, project, organization, or person.

CHAPTER 6

*Where there is no vision,
the people perish.
–Proverbs 29:18*

CHAPTER 6

The Payoff Question
What Does Success Look Like?

The payoff is the desired end state or vision and answers the question, what does success look like?

Like in the previous chapter, this is another wonderful opportunity to lead the team in a discussion, get insight into how others are thinking, and see how aligned the team really is.

A good exercise is to begin by asking everyone to again record their ideas, but this time on what success looks like. The question forces everyone to consider a specific outcome. It lets you know if everyone is looking at the effort in the same way. Phrased another way, what is the clear benefit to whom?

Leading the team discussion on payoff is a great opportunity to brainstorm with the team about success because success means different things to different people. Different people will have different payoffs and that allows some review of different payoff options. As a leader, you need to bring everyone together under one common payoff.

Here are additional questions to confirm you are getting to the right answers about payoff:

Is the answer to the question specific and clear?

Does it say we will do exactly this?

What is the desired end state?

Is it relevant to the challenge?

Do we have a consensus on realistic measurements for success?

Does it respond to or solve the problem before us?

Is the answer future-focused? Delivered by when?

Are the answers values-driven?

Is it inspiring for all?

You can ensure the answers provided will specifically identify the payoff by following the SMART formula for goal setting.

Specific

Be specific about what the payoff is. Capture all available details because they may prove valuable in the future. Quality is a good example. You may start by wanting something that is ninety-nine per cent accurate, but once the project is underway, a quality level of ninety-five percent accurate may be adequate.

Measurable

How do you measure success? What is the yardstick? Will it be consistent year over year?

Achievable

Is the payoff challenging but not impossible? This is the concept of stretch goals popular in sales positions. For example, there should be enough sales revenue to make budget and just a little more.

Relevant

Is the payoff answer purpose-driven? Does it respond to our why?

Time bound

All benchmarks and achievements are bound or due by a specific date.

Of particular importance is the relevancy and whether the payoff is purpose-driven (does it fit with our purpose and answer our why?).

This is where a lot of projects can get misaligned from the beginning or drift off course. To be blunt, the what doesn't work for the why. The successful future state identified will not address the reason we are here.

If the answer to the question about what success looks like does not fully answer the first question about why we are here, then you are on the wrong track. There is no point going any further because the payoff does not fully address the purpose.

As a leader, you must know the answer to this question of what success looks like cold. Visualize the specific benefits and achievements. Everyone needs to know where they are going and the ultimate payoff. Usually there is one big payoff and several smaller ones. Acknowledge that this big payoff is the target everyone is reaching for and reinforce that vision whenever possible.

Everyone needs to agree to the payoffs because it creates a point of unity and commitment with the team. Sometimes this commitment is demonstrated by team members being asked to literally sign off on the vision. Participants sign their name as a physical representation of their commitment to the project.

> *To be a leader, you have to make people want to follow you, and nobody wants to follow someone who doesn't know where he is going.*[44]
> *–Joe Namath, 1969 Super Bowl champion*

KEY LESSON

Question two, what does success look like? is the vision statement that describes the payoff, the target, or the future desired state.

Use the SMART formula to drill down and be detailed about what your payoff will be.

CREATE THE PLAN

CHAPTER 7

*You don't get results by focusing on results,
you get results by focusing on the actions that
produce results.*
–Mike Hawkins, Others: Developing People

CHAPTER 7

The Process Question
How Do We Get There?

Before we decide on what processes are required to produce the desired payoff, we need to acknowledge that the first step in any project is to understand the decision-making authority. This begins with identifying who holds the authority to make decisions because this can influence the processes generated.

Does the authority lie within the team or is it external to the group, such as a supervisor or a board? Is it one person or a group of decision makers? Who will decide and how often is their direction required? Who presents to the authority and how often?

It is of particular importance to the team dynamics that the decision-making authority is established upfront.

Does this authority decide by simple majority or super majority, or does the decision ultimately rest with an individual with a veto? Is that veto in the room? How many are needed for quorum to make a binding decision?

All of these influences need to be discussed to ensure they are adequately accounted for within the processes. For example, would the decision maker need to approve phases as they are achieved or do they wait for the final product?

Once the authority is identified and communicated to the team, an examination of the processes required can begin. This is the overall plan broken down into all the different processes.

> *If you don't know where you are going,*
> *you will end up some place else.*[45]
> *−Yogi Berra*

While it is easiest to have one payoff, sometimes other ones arise. For every payoff identified, there will be a process or several processes to achieve that goal. These processes need to be documented for every payoff desired. The resulting task list that gets developed is very similar to the work breakdown structure that you may have seen in project management training. You are trying to capture everything required, so use every tool you have, such as process mapping, Gantt charts, Venn diagrams—whatever you can use to record the necessary steps to success. Quantify these steps as much as possible.

In large projects, it is not uncommon for there to be several payoffs and several processes developed as the project moves from the executive ranks down to departments and managers, and finally to each employee. Each list of activities will get more specific as they get downloaded to the next level and eventually attached to each employee.

Sub-plans can handle the depth of detail required for larger projects. For example, the marketing department may have to develop the strategic plan, but within the strategic plan, there may be many other plans that rest underneath, such as market research, sales canvases, advertising campaigns, and social media. This would, of course, necessitate additional accountability matrices for each area.

> *The secret of all victory lies in the*
> *organization of the nonobvious.* [46]
> *−Marcus Aurelius*

The required commitment of all affected stakeholders is usually obtained at this time through consultation and presentations. It is critical to share the purpose and payoff obtained in questions one and two to obtain agreement from the team and collect their ideas on what they need to proceed. How we get there is a question for the team to develop and build from the ground up, not from the top down.

Team discussions at this point should be around the different options for the processes available. There are several paths to get to your goal, and the options of each will have trade-offs in one of three ways.

> **Quality factors:** effective quality increases or cost-saving de creases
>
> **Time factors:** speed to market, suppliers schedule, turnaround
>
> **Financial factors:** increased revenues or decreased costs

Depending on your why (purpose), you may want to examine each of these factors and how they may affect the payoff you desire. Your job with the team is to settle on the best process to achieve the payoff.

At this point, refrain from assigning responsibilities (this will be discussed in the next module). You are only looking to capture processes and feedback on the activities (i.e., Will these activities get us there?).

If you begin to assign responsibilities, individuals will change their focus to their own goals and what it will take them to be successful. Once they know what they must do, individuals can lose the bigger picture for their own perspective. They usually move from thinking about the overall goals to what they personally will need to do to be successful.

> *Never tell people how to do things.*
> *Tell them what to do and they will*
> *surprise you with their ingenuity.*[47]
> –George S. Patton, American WW II general

Again, remember to consider corporate values and company culture when developing the processes required to achieve your payoff. If you are perusing a project that could affect your values, you will need to contemplate all the ramifications. There are always risks attached to any changes to corporate values, so ensure you carefully consider and mitigate the risks.

CREATE THE PLAN

Finally, throughout the project, challenge the team to ensure their activities and processes are moving the project toward the intended payoffs. Without ongoing reinforcement, the people's focus and even the targets themselves can change and things will quickly move from order to chaos

KEY LESSON

The question of how we get there begins with who decides where "there" is. Who really decides what success looks like. There is always an authority who needs to be included in the process because their approval and sign-off indicate the project is on the right track. Updates on the project's progress will need to be created and delivered to this authority.

Question three, how do we get there? identifies all the processes (but not the people) required for successful implementation of the plan and for the desired payoff to be achieved.

PART 2

CHAPTER 8

*To understand the true quality of people,
you must look into their minds, and
examine their pursuits and aversions.
–Marcus Aurelius*

CHAPTER 8

The People Question
Who Does What, When?

The question of who does what, when is really a question about personalities.

To put your team's strengths to work, you must first know what they are good at and what they are not. It is only natural that certain people have the right skills and are good at certain jobs, but what about weaknesses, which most individuals will generally hide? What if you are a new leader and they are not familiar with the team? How can you quickly understand the team to gain trust?

To answer these questions, this chapter deals with people in a general sense; later in the book, we will closely review different people and their personalities, and how you can capitalize on each by playing to their strengths.

Great leaders know people. They understand the team and the dynamics within the team.

As Peter Drucker said, leaders "orchestrate the energy," and in some dismal cases, leaders must first create that energy themselves. If you are in an environment where energy, enthusiasm, and passion are missing, it is up to you as leader to create some and build it within the team.

> *The growth and development of people
> is the highest calling of leadership.*[48]
> *–Harvey S. Firestone, American businessman*

When it comes to people management, great leaders know or understand four key dynamics for the growth and development of their people.

1. Leaders understand themselves.

Great leaders know where they are strong and where they are weak and will hire accordingly to address their shortcomings. For example, if a particular leader is weak in IT, they should hire an IT professional to fill that gap. In the same way, great leaders also try to choose diverse, even opposing, personalities to ensure a rich team mix. This may seem counterintuitive, but a rich mix in a team's personalities generally makes a better team.

I was doing some consulting work for a board and despite my best intentions, the members just couldn't seem to reach consensus and make a decision. They often delayed important decisions, and timely opportunities were passing them by.

It was frustrating to all on the board, and staff were becoming disillusioned about the leadership.

I had the board's personalities tested and the profiles evaluated. Interestingly, all were the same type, and their cautious and methodical approach increased exponentially when they met as a group. They had in time become so cautious that the risks always outweighed the opportunity.

Soon after, they expanded their membership with more risk-tolerant personalities and the board generated many profitable opportunities.

The lesson here is that similar personalities tend to close in on themselves, causing a heightening of that personality's characteristics. For example, a room full of extroverts will have even more energy than normal, as they try to outdo each other.

2. Leaders understand each of the individuals in the team.

Great leaders know each member of the team, and they often maintain some unique reinforcing connection with each individual member. This can often be quite subtle but enormously effective. For example, I once had a great leader who spent part of every Monday morning going around and connecting with most of his 250 employees, just asking how their weekend was and whatever happened to…?

He was a genuine person, who knew everyone's background and where they were in each of their lives. Everyone loved him and he was universally known as a great guy.

The staff loyalty he created was incredibly strong and was fully demonstrated when the stress increased and deadlines were looming. Everyone had to work on weekends and happily jumped in.

A great leader once said to me, "Your team will talk about you at their dining room table, and you control what they say." Many years later, one of my dearest staff mentioned, "I was talking about what you last night at dinner with my husband." I smiled as I remembered the sage comment from years earlier.

The question you want to ask yourself, if you want to be a leader is, what do you want them saying about you at their dining room table?

3. Leaders understand the dynamics within the team.

Great leaders keep a constant watch on the team and the interactions between members. They understand teams may take years to bond but can break in a moment. The more passionate a team is, the more likely conflict will arise, and managing that can be challenging yet beneficial.

Most newly assembled teams go through a series of clear phases that include forming, storming, norming, and performing.[49] You will experience these phases every time a new team is formed.

I am amazed at how these phases always arise and how distinct they are. As a leader, you must understand these phases and know what phase your team is in. True performance occurs when everything is settled and everyone is comfortable with their roles and each other. The results can then be exponentially delivered.

4. Leaders understand the dynamics between the team and others.

Often it is the high-profile team that will endure the most scrutiny. For this reason, it is critical for the leader to continuously reinforce the value of their team externally and highlight the important work they are delivering. Memories are mighty short and corporate jealousies are a real thing. As the leader, you are the cheerleader for every member of your team and need to help each of them to have what Brandy Halladay would refer to as "perfect moments."

> *People are not perfect. We all struggle.*
> *But with hard work, humility, and dedication,*
> *imperfect people can still have perfect moments.*[50]
> *–Brandy Halladay (widow of Roy Halladay)*

KEY LESSON

The answer to question four, who does what, when? ties the individuals required for success to the tasks identified in chapter seven (How do we get there?).

In order to successfully assign individuals to tasks, it would be extremely beneficial to understand the individuals on the team and what motivates them. For that reason, we will return to personalities for further study in chapters thirteen to seventeen.

CHAPTER 9

Critique, feedback, reactions to one's work or the way they have presented it, regardless of intentions, is a gift.
–Mark Brand, Canadian chef

CHAPTER 9

The Performance Question
How Are You Doing?

The first four questions represent the core of the accountability matrix, but we need to add two more questions for individual performances and progress on corporate goals.

> *That which gets measured, gets done.*[51]
> *–Georg Joachim Rheticus*

Following the people question is question five, How are you doing? This is a key performance question, but it is really asking two things: How are you doing today (your mood, for example) and How are you doing on your projects?

How are you doing today? is an attempt to check on the wellbeing and attitude of that team member on that day.

As mentioned, smart leaders keep up with their team members' individual activities. They keep tabs on how the staff are doing and what is important in their life. (If you can't remember what your team is passionate about, at least write it down somewhere.)

For example, if you know they ski, ask them how often they managed to get to the mountains. Try to connect with what they do and why they do it.

Remember their personality preference and approach them appropriately (more material on personality profiles begins with chapter thirteen).

Secondly, you can ask them how they are doing on their projects.

Now is the time for them to raise any challenges they may have with timing, quality, or financials. I have found success by engaging in management by walking around, just like my previous president.

I spent the first part of Monday mornings just walking around and saying good morning to everyone. I asked what they were up to on the weekend and then what they hoped to accomplish this week. A simple What is on your schedule this week? can open up some important dialogue, which may not otherwise be raised.

As a leader, you have numerous tools you can employ, but some of your most powerful tools are the words you choose and how you say them. At some point, you will have to deliver bad news, corrective measures, or oversee an outright departure (voluntary or otherwise). Words matter and how you deliver them matters. Tone, pace, inflection, and body language all influence how the message is received, so be cognizant of their impact.

Giving negative feedback is never easy, but if you remember to be firm, friendly, and fair, you should make the conversation a little easier for all.

1. Firm, in that you need to be very clear about the behaviour in question, rigid about the boundaries involved, and succinct about the repercussions.
2. Friendly, in that you don't necessarily need to be adversarial. Don't make tough conversations more difficult by creating a me-versus-you scenario. The situation may well devolve to that, but you as leader should not be the one to take it there.
3. Fair, in that you are fair and reasonable to all concerned. This is one of the four-way tests used by Rotary International (thank you, Rotary!), but it is obviously valuable in daily practice.[52]

One final technique about how to use words and phrases to help you connect to your people: if you want to understand someone's gut reaction to something, ask, "I value your thoughts here; how do you feel about all of this?" They will usually provide their initial or gut reaction.

If you want to understand someone's intellectual reaction to something, ask, "I value your thoughts here; what do you think about this?" Here, you are literally asking them to think. They will usually take a minute to formulate an logical answer because they subconsciously want to appear intelligent.

> *All that is valuable in human society depends upon the opportunity for development accorded the individual.*[53]
> –Albert Einstein

KEY LESSON

Question five centers on feedback and follows up on the individual performances by asking, how are you doing? The question, however, can also be used to politely probe how they are doing emotionally and what else they have been up to outside of work. The team member may not respond, but just asking the question indicates you care about them beyond work hours. These casual and random dialogues may seem inconsequential, but they do help bond the team.

CHAPTER 10

*I think it's very important to have a feedback loop,
where you're constantly thinking about what
you've done
and how you could be doing it better.
–Elon Musk*

CHAPTER 10

The Progress Question
How Are We Doing?

I once worked for an organization that had a twenty-seven-page annual review that usually took an individual a day or so to write. The subsequent review with HR and their immediate supervisor took easily another two hours. Once completed, the reviews were utilized for performance reviews. It was all very formal and intimidating. Beside the time involved, the process significantly rattled the staff with stress. I took exception and asked the president, "Why don't we measure what matters?"

Some organizations, like this one, like to measure everything, but that is a nice-to-have with questionable value. Measuring what matters is critical if the overall corporate goals are to be achieved. The last question of the six is about how we are doing as a team or company. The overall corporate goals are dependant on all the previously identified individual processes being successfully implemented. These corporate goals are built on the collective results of the entire team, and team members need to know that. The team needs to know how their actions in attempting to reach their goals build up to the corporate level. However, if you are measuring the wrong criteria (or every possible criterion), your corporate goals will be way off. You are utilizing a shotgun when you really need a rifle.

Successful individual goals are small yet vital incremental steps toward overall corporate success. The answers to question six will form the building blocks for the overall corporate achievements, but how do you really know how you are doing?

> *Progress lies not in enhancing what is,*
> *but in advancing toward what will be.*[54]
> –Khalil Gibran, Lebanese American writer, poet, painter

Financial performance is the standard because you can measure the profitability and all the typical margins (gross, operating, net, etc.), but these are just a recap of past performance.

For deeper understanding, you can try benchmarking your financials, customer service, and even employees against the industry standards. This normally yields valuable information, but again, these measures are looking into the past.

How do we begin to see and understand our future? The answer is simple—just ask.

Every time I began a new position, I began with informal market research, and it usually began with the present employees. I interviewed them about what was working, what was not working, and what they would change if they were in my position.

Then I casually interviewed key customers to understand their why. If I could understand why they are there (chapter five), it would help me to understand why they do business with us.

Next, I sought customers who were not presently with us and tried to find out why. The answers on why they did not do business with us was always insightful, punishingly accurate, and sometimes humbling (usually due to an unaddressed error on our part).

I have even attended hiring fairs to discuss the company with young students, hoping to understand how potential employees view our company. These insights help shape future branding efforts and messaging. Again, as outlined in the previous chapter, you want their gut reaction, so the first question should be, how do you feel about company X?"

You can follow that up with the "what do you think?" question but then you cannot go back to gut feelings. Try to get the feelings before the thoughts.

This approach will give you their initial perception and any positive or negative feelings they may have. Ensure you share the feedback with the team to see if the observations are valid to them. Your team will always comment on these observations, thereby providing further feedback for you to consider.

I encourage you as a leader to do this research regularly, as your market and perceptions about your company (or team) change regularly.

In chapter seven we discussed the identification of the decision maker as the authority who is ultimately championing the effort. We have now gone full circle because the answer here on how we are doing is targeted for that authority.

KEY LESSON

Question six asks, How are we doing? and is really asking the big-picture question, How are we doing in reaching our overall or corporate goals?

The answer can be somewhat subjective because the overall progress is dependent on successfully delivering on all the individual goals. These individual goals will not be delivered at the same time, so your must balance your answer with the likelihood of delivery on all those individual efforts.

CREATE THE PLAN

CHAPTER 11

Any valuable "creative idea" must always be logical in hindsight (after it has been seen). If the idea were not logical with hindsight, then we would never be able to see the value of the idea.

Ideas that are not logical in hindsight remain as "mad" ideas. They may be mad forever or only until we catch up with the paradigm change.

–Edward de Bono, Maltese author

CHAPTER 11

Applying the Full Accountability Matrix

Here is the fully assembled accountability matrix with the six questions. The top three boxes have a company-wide focus and flow effectively into each other from left to right with. With the progress question, you are tracking overall efforts, and this usually occurs last because the individual results begin to come in.

Figure 10. The Results Matter Accountability Matrix

1. PURPOSE Why are we here?	2. PAYOFF What does success look like?	6. PROGRESS How are we doing?
3. PROCESS How do we get there?	4. PEOPLE Who does what, when?	5. PERFORMANCE How are you doing?

The bottom three boxes break the project down into individual efforts and as previously mentioned, track the team's individual performances and monitor results. Exceptions and changes can and should be noted under the performance module, as these changes can affect other deliverables.

The numbers indicate the order the matrix is to be completed.

I would like to provide you with two examples of the Results Matter accountability matrix in operation and will begin with the relatively simple example of weight loss.

In chapter twelve, I will provide a more complex onboarding example.

The Weight-Loss Accountability Matrix Example

As previously stated, the matrix can be used in a variety of applications. I chose weight loss because of its universality (who could not benefit from losing a few pounds?), as well as the growing severity of obesity in society today.

In the United States, seventy per cent of the population over the age of twenty is overweight or obese. Before the rest of the world gets too smug, I would also note that obesity rates have tripled worldwide.[55]

What follows here is a simple example of how an individual could use the accountability matrix for a weight-loss program.

Figure 11. Six Questions for a Weight-Loss Program

1. PURPOSE	2. PAYOFF	6. PROGRESS
Why are we here?	What does success look like?	How are we doing?
To lose 20 lb in 90 days	1. Better health 2. Good looks 3. Improved strength/balance	• TBD • TBD • TBD

3. PROCESS	4. PEOPLE	5. PERFORMANCE
How do we get there?	Who does what, when?	How are you doing?
• Health check • Healthy food/vitamins • Regular workout • Regular walk	• Dr. Kildare • Dietician • Gym coach • Friend	• Check up okay (date) • Started (date) • Next week (date) • Started (date)

In this example, the purpose question of why we are here is answered with, to lose twenty pounds in ninety days. The payoff (What does success look like?) is better health, better looks, and improved strength and balance. In this example, we have purposely left the overall progress as "to be decided," but you may use weekly weigh-ins to track overall progress.

To achieve this weight-loss goal, you may engage a doctor (to approve the exercise program), a dietician for meals, a gym coach for exercise, and a friend for walks to keep you sane through all of this.

Notice how your performance (individual efforts) and progress (toward overall goal) are easily tracked and you can even decide under what time frames.

CHAPTER 12

*If you are lucky enough to be someone's employer,
then you have a moral obligation to make sure people
do look forward to coming to work in the morning.
—John Mackey, CEO, Whole Foods*

CHAPTER 12

The Onboarding Accountability Matrix

The beauty of Results Matter is its universality, where it can be utilized for any personal project, group project, strategic planning, and virtually any performance management effort. It has even proven valuable for corporate visioning exercises. Over time, you will discover and benefit from the many different uses of this methodology.

In this chapter, I wanted to provide a more complex example of the Results Matter approach and walk through the matrix question by question.

I chose onboarding for my second example because it is one of my biggest HR pet peeves. Poor onboarding costs businesses millions of dollars every year. Research shows that about thirty per cent of all businesses do not even maintain an onboarding plan. An effective onboarding plan, as provided here, results in greater retention, faster productivity, and—over time—greater productivity.

Research from 2015 demonstrates just how critical onboarding can be. Twenty-five per cent of new hires leave in the first year. The total cost of that turnover can range from one hundred per cent to three hundred per cent of that individual's annual salary, and it takes about six to eight months for a new employee to start producing results.[56]

The Oxford Dictionary of Human Resource Management (3 ed.) defines onboarding as the process from when a candidate first contacts an organization through to when they become an established employee.[57]

I would describe onboarding as the organizational chemistry that occurs between the new hire and the company. Onboarding involves the three objectives of orientation, expectations, and accreditation—but first, let us start the six questions and be clear about why we are here.

Populating the Accountability Matrix

We will begin with the original matrix and populate it by answering the key questions outlined below.

Figure 12. The Results Matter Accountability Matrix

PURPOSE Why are we here?	**PAYOFF** What does success look like?	**PROGRESS** How are we doing?
PROCESS How do we get there?	**PEOPLE** Who does what, when?	**PERFORMANCE** How are you doing?

As we complete the matrix, please refer to figure 13 and follow how the details are collected and the matrix filled out.

Question one: *Why are we here (purpose)?*

In our onboarding example, our purpose is to successfully onboard a new employee. Ideally, we want to help the new employee to "hit the ground running," and we use this module to clarify and ensure that every individual involved in this onboarding objective understands why we are here.

For our onboarding example, our why is to onboard a new employee and it is entered into the matrix (see figure 13)

Question two: *What does success look like (payoff)?*

Next is to identify the eventual payoff by answering the question, What does success look like? As previously mentioned with this example, there are three payoffs with our purpose of onboarding a new employee.

PAYOFF ONE – ORIENTATION: We want to introduce the new employee to the organization and orient them to the company's unique culture.

PAYOFF TWO – EXPECTATIONS: We want to communicate the position's responsibilities and establish the performance expectations.

PAYOFF THREE – ACCREDITATION: We want to quickly establish the employee's accreditation and thereby establish their access to the company's resources.

These three payoffs of orientation, expectations and accreditation are listed on the matrix (see figure 13).

Question three is about how we get there, and we begin by looking at the first payoff of orientation.

We are now ready to identify all the processes required to achieve these three payoffs by answering the question, *How do we get there?*

Here, as previously indicated, it is important to outline the steps required but not the individuals who will take the tasks. Remember, establish the tasks first and assign responsibilities to these tasks later.

The tasks don't change much, but the individual can change because of many factors. The matrix is created to easily move around the individuals responsible for each task, if required.

In our example, the orientation includes the initial welcome and an education on the company's history, common norms, competitive positioning, marketing strategies, and approach to the market. It may also include things such as a welcoming function or reception, welcome emails, distribution of company premiums, company clothing, standard uniforms, or whatever you have that makes them feel part of the new team. We will capture these activities on the matrix under, How do we get there (process)? and under orientation as welcome.

CREATE THE PLAN

The next activity under orientation is the provisioning of an early schedule, usually covering the first one-to-three days. The new hire is usually shopped around the office and introduced. They may get some job shadowing with key employees. They will receive all the relevant company information, which can take the form of position descriptions, organizational charts, different department meetings, minutes or even site tours. The direction of the team and the roles of the various team members can be detailed. These activities will be added to the matrix under schedule (and remember, this is only for the first one-to-three days).

Next are policies and procedures that are normal with every hire. This can take the form of everything from safety and first aid policies, emergency procedures, and legal restrictions to HR requirements, such as payroll and benefits. These activities will be described on the matrix under orientation as policies.

The last activity under orientation is housekeeping, which includes all the legal and HR paperwork required when you start a new job—things such as payroll deposit, government paperwork, agreed deductions, and credit cards. This is added to the matrix as paperwork.

Continuing with question three, we will now look at how we get there for the expectations and accreditation payoffs.

The next major payoff is that of expectations, and this one is critical but often missed. Activities need to be developed early and agreed to for thirty, sixty, and ninety days. What will success look like in the next one, two, and three months? In this way, both the employer and the new hire fully understand the expectations that come with the position. Typically, the first ninety days are a probationary period, where both parties have time to see if there is a strategic fit between them.

Once we establish clear activities for thirty, sixty, and ninety days, we enter them into the matrix under expectations as 30, 60, and 90.

Key performance indicators (or KPIs) remove any doubt over what success looks like. The KPIs are essentially the goals established for the position. Not only should key targets be agreed to, but the method of measurement must be identified. This discussion and the agreements on goals and the methods of measurement that are established are indicated on the matrix as KPIs.

Besides these concrete KPIs, it is critical to ensure an understanding about some of the organization's more subtle norms, such as the type of culture promoted and the company values. Remember that both the culture and the values may not be immediately evident to a new hire. For the matrix, we will enter this activity as values.

Finally, some time should be spent establishing expectations around career development and promotions. While some employees will be happy to stay in their current position, every employee will appreciate hearing there is potential to grow with the company. With this activity, various career paths are outlined and usually some idea of the training required to advance. I will refer to this as culture.

The accreditation payoff involves ensuring the new hire gets both physical and electronic access to the organization's assets. Physical access involves security access to the building, the office, and the parking, while electronic access involves items such as network access, company intranet, remote access from home, and hardware such as laptops, cell phones, and other devices.

For our example here, I have included all these access activities on the matrix as accreditation in figure 13.

We now move to question four, *who does what, when?*

Question four (the people question) involves deploying your team to the tasks identified in question three. In this section, we look to place people best suited for completing that task.

Returning to our onboarding example, we assign an individual to be responsible for each process identified to achieve that payoff. For example, under orientation, an HR advisor would typically deal with the company welcome, the early schedule, all the polices and procedures, and the housekeeping and paperwork.

Under expectations, the required activities are listed and we will assume that direction is coming from one person—the VP of sales.

CREATE THE PLAN

For the accreditation portion, we will assign those tasks to the IT lead (figure 13).

Note how we add the completion date or due date in parentheses behind the name of the individual responsible.

And now the fun part starts, where we can begin to track results. But before we go there, let's review what we have created thus far.

In figure 13, the top row identifies the corporate goals, while the bottom row contains the individual goals and time frames for each. On the top, we have our purpose and payoff, and on the bottom, we have process and people. On the right side, we have question six, how are we doing (progress on the company goals)? and underneath that question five, how are you doing (performance on the individual goals)? This order of questions five and six makes sense because individual goals build up and towards overall corporate goals.

Question five introduces individual performances with, *how are you doing?*

The matrix is now filled out with the individual assignments required for that specific onboarding effort, and we can track each individual performance as it moves toward that goal. The status of each individual team member is reflected under performance.

In our example, the values and culture tasks have yet to be completed. As indicated, the VP went out of town.

Moving to question six, we are now ready to see how we are progressing on the overall goal with, *how are we doing?*

Once we begin to see individual results, we can begin to track progress on corporate results. In our example, individual results roll up to the corporate goals and, as you can see, some did not get completed.

Figure 13. The Completed Onboarding Matrix

1. PURPOSE	2. PAYOFF	6. PROGRESS
Why are we here?	What does success look like?	How are we doing?
To onboard a new employee	1. Orientation 2. Expectations 3. Accreditation	1. Completed Jan 17 • OUTSTANDING 2. Completed Jan 17

3. PROCESS	4. PEOPLE	5. PERFORMANCE
How do we get there?	Who does what, when?	How are you doing?
1. Orientation		
• Welcome	• HR (Jan. 15)	• Completed Jan. 15
• Schedule	• HR (Jan. 15)	• Completed Jan. 15
• Policies	• HR (Jan. 16)	• Completed Jan. 16
• Paperwork	• HR (Jan. 16)	• Completed Jan. 17
2. Expectations		
• 30, 60, 90	• VP Sales (Jan. 17)	• Completed Jan. 17
• KPIs	• VP Sales (Jan. 17)	• Completed Jan. 17
• Values	• VP Sales (Jan. 17)	• OUTSTANDING (VP out of town)
• Culture	• VP Sales (Jan. 17)	• OUTSTANDING
3. Accreditation	• IT Lead (Jan. 15)	• Completed Jan. 17

What we have profiled with our onboarding example is a complete accountability matrix that has several benefits.

The matrix speaks to all stakeholders at all levels, so everyone should be on the same page.

The matrix clearly communicates both the individual and the corporate goals for this effort.

The matrix assigns responsibilities and time frames.

CREATE THE PLAN

The matrix tracks the performance of both the individuals and the organization.

I have provided a complete and detailed onboarding checklist in the appendix for your future use.

Your matrix is now complete and will serve as a blueprint for your successful onboarding. You have created a dynamic document that you can circulate, change, and update with the team as the project (in this case, onboarding) progresses.

Results Matter online (resultsmatter.app)

The above examples are fairly simple, but life (and business) can get pretty hectic, so I understand when paper applications may not work as well; I created an online collaborative platform called Results Matter (resultsmatter.app), where this entire accountability matrix is automated and online.

At the Results Matter site, you can create, edit, share, circulate, and store your own accountability matrix.

In the online version, I created a traffic light system, so you can quickly review and identify changes or challenges with that process or individual. You can easily change the traffic lights with a click, and there is an opportunity to include further explanation.

I explain the breakdown of the different colours of the traffic lights below, but you can always create your own definitions for your own individual needs:

If the traffic light is green, everything is proceeding according to plan.

If the traffic light is yellow, there are material changes or delays you need to know about.

If the traffic light is red, there is a fundamental issue that requires your attention.

KEY LESSON

The onboarding example provided above is a good demonstration of a simple application. My intent was to show how the questions flow; however, it begins to test the physical limits of a paper product and can quickly become too cumbersome. For most applications, the website at resultsmatter.app is usually a better choice.

PART 3

Focus The Team

*If two people are exactly alike,
one of them would be unnecessary.*
–Larry Dixon, Jr., American racing driver

CHAPTER 13

Introduction to Personality Profiles

Now that we have a plan established with our six questions, we can examine the team members in greater detail to understand exactly who should do what, when (question four).

Personalities matter because they can boost a project or quickly derail one. As a leader, it is critical that you understand people and what motivates them.

This chapter begins with two exercises you can try, but it is imperative to follow the instructions. Please read the entire exercise before beginning the exercise.

Exercise one

Close your eyes and imagine yourself in front of a whiteboard. You are standing about a foot and a half away. As you stare at it, you can see some of the old marks and letters not quite wiped away. You reach down and pick up a blue marker. As you take the cap off, you smell the chemicals from the ink.

Now I want you to imagine writing your signature on the whiteboard. Sign it as if you are signing your name on a contract. Write it in the air in front of you right now.

Write your full name about a foot high.

Can you see it on the whiteboard?

How does it look?

Exercise two

Now we are going to try it again, but with one small difference.

Begin by closing your eyes. Imagine yourself in front of a whiteboard again, about a foot and a half away. You reach down and pick up a blue marker. As you take the cap off, you smell the chemicals from the ink.

Now I want you to imagine writing your signature on the whiteboard, only this time I want you to use your other hand to sign.

Do not hesitate! Sign your full name again, but this time use the other hand. Again, about a foot tall. You can open your eyes…

How did that feel?

How do you imagine that would look?

The first time you signed with your usual hand, you found it natural and effortless, and you didn't have to even think about it. If you could see the signature, it would appear relatively consistent and "adult."

The second time, when you used your other hand, you would probably describe the attempt as awkward, unnatural, and clumsy. You may have had to concentrate more and, if you could see the end result, it would likely appear messy and "child-like."

Personality preferences are a lot like this handwriting exercise.

While there are many personality traits, we develop preferences for some over time. Think of personality traits as our preferences or habits in how we approach the world.

A personality preference is effortless and natural, just like writing with your dominant hand. It is not that you can't sign your name with the other hand; it is just a bit awkward and not your first choice.

You have a natural personality style as well, where you don't have to think about your approach and everything just flows.

Personality types are generally very consistent over time; however, you may demonstrate a different personality type because of several factors. Pressures from work and culture, family, physical health, mental health, and finances can all cause stress that results in some short-term variations in your style and behaviour. Once the crisis has passed, however, people move back to their original style.

Try to think of personalities like a set of hats.

- I often wear that hat (seventy per cent of the time)
- I sometimes wear that hat (twenty-five per cent of the time)
- I rarely wear that hat (five per cent of the time)
- I never wear that hat (zero per cent of the time)

Personalities are similar and under closer self-examination, most people typically find the following.

- I often demonstrate that personality type (seventy per cent of the time)
- I sometimes demonstrate that personality type (twenty-five per cent of the time)
- I rarely demonstrate that personality type (five per cent of the time)
- I never demonstrate that personality type (zero per cent of the time)

Each personality profile has both good and bad aspects, so there are no right or wrong answers to a personality test. With personality styles, you are not looking at a test of absolutes; rather, it is a test of preferences. Behaviours that happen most of the time but not all of the time.

FOCUS THE TEAM

92 *INTRODUCTION TO PERSONALITY PROFILES*

I would suggest that a rich mix of personalities makes for a better team than one in which the team is all one personality type. All one personality type tends to reinforce each others' proclivities, and this can easily overwhelm one perspective.

> *There are many kinds of leaders.*
> *Too often we confuse a forceful personality*
> *with leadership. This is a mistake.*
> *Those with different talents and styles can*
> *reach the same mountain top. They*
> *just take different roads to get there.*[58]
> –Henry H. Neff, American author

There are no perfect matches and no one is exclusively one type, so personality profiles rest on a best-fit approach.

Further, personality profiles are not one hundred per cent accurate, but the stronger the personality, the more predictive the behaviour. For our purposes here, we will examine the very strong personalities that exist at the extremes to reveal the behaviours being discussed. Personalities will cluster around certain traits and most fall within a bell curve distribution.[59] Humans are complex, especially when it comes to personalities, but these personality clusters tend to be consistent over time.

To be clear, I suggest that attempting to change the attributes of a leader may be effective for four to six weeks (at best), but most people will quickly return to their natural personality.

Figure 14. Personality Profile Distribution

15%   35%   35%   *Extremes*   15%

LESS EVIDENT ⟵ **TRAITS** ⟶ **MORE EVIDENT**

PART 3

Like many things, personality profiles exist on a bell curve, with most people occupying the middle seventy to eighty per cent.

People are more than their type, but it is only one of many ways to look at motivations and group dynamics. For our purposes, we will look at four general types (out of thousands of possible types, depending on the criteria used).

By examining each personality in greater detail, we can uncover how they get their energy (introversion/extroversion) and where they focus most of that energy (on a people orientation or a process/project orientation).

KEY LESSON

I am often amazed how little aspiring leaders know about personality profiles and yet, they are your most valuable tool. As a leader, you need to know your own personality profile in great detail and how that will integrate with the rest of the team. Personality types create profiles that help you understand and predict group dynamics and individual motivations. In the next five chapters, we will introduce each of the four personality profiles and what drives them.

CHAPTER 14

Everybody is somebody's weirdo.
—Scott Adams, cartoonist

CHAPTER 14

There Are Only Four Types of People

As we saw in chapter one, leadership begins with the balance between authority and enlightenment (push and pull) but leadership is much more complex than that.

In that earlier example, we only had two variables (authority versus reason), which made the personality types fairly simple. By adding two more variables, the resulting types become more detailed, more complex, and therefore more applicable in a work environment. This increased detail allows for greater accuracy and predictability of behaviours.

For thousands of years, it has been thought that there are four types of people in the world. This theory began with the father of medicine, Hippocrates, who first identified the four types or "humours," and most modern-day personality models follow his original work.[60]

It wasn't until 1875 that Carl Jung took the idea of personality much further and defined the theories. Then around 1944, Isabel Myers and Katharine Briggs developed the profiles and the tests.[61]

Today, many of the personality profiles are developed and strengthened from this initial work by Myers and Briggs. Over the last eighty years, many different approaches have been based on the original four, but I have also seen new themes based on types of colours, animals, birds, hats, even trees.

There is even one type of personality profile that is based on the chemical subsystems in the brain. The Fisher Temperament Inventory is based on the idea that behaviour is influenced by the dominance of certain neurotransmitters in the brain. The four types include testosterone (~Drivers), estrogen (~Amiables), dopamine (~Expressives) and serotonin (~Thinkers).[62]

Great leaders can see how we interact with the world and the motivations of ourselves and others. Some have this insight naturally and others have developed it.

Personality profiles provide an essential framework for understanding where people are coming from.

I have implemented personality profiles as fun icebreakers with every new team I've worked with and found that the cohesion and alignment occurred much faster as a result.

> *If everyone is thinking alike, then someone isn't thinking.*[63]
> *–George S. Patton, American general*

For ease of your understanding, I will use below a simplified version of the Merrill and Reid model because the model directly outlines two key personality criteria of leadership.[64]

If we distill leadership to its core, we see only two high-level responsibilities for every leader.

>ENERGY—Develop and orchestrate the team's energy.

>FOCUS—Focus the team's energy appropriately.

Energy and focus go a long way in setting the different personalities of your team, so these are the two personality criteria we will use in our profiles.

Specifically, we will look at two questions: Where do you get your energy and where do you focus your energy? The answers to these two questions will generate four distinct personality types.

Energy

Roughly seventy percent of people are Introverts and Introverts are the ones who stay home after a hard week. They are more reserved and generally quieter than most. Introverts are very cerebral because they tend to pick their words carefully and think before they speak.

The other thirty per cent are the people who would go out, gather socially, and have dinner and drinks with friends. These are the extroverts, and they are all about getting their energy and recharging though others. They are outgoing, highly social, and talkative. They are terribly busy with many projects at one time.

Focus

The next criterion we will examine is where people focus their energy. Essentially, you are looking at whether they are project-focused or people-focused.

The project-focused are very analytical and tough-minded, and value everything being fair and equal. They decide according to logical facts and are known for deciding with their head, but at the extreme they can be labelled as heartless.

The people-focused are gentle and sympathetic, and value harmony above all else. They decide according to their own values and norms and generally decide with their heart. At the extreme, they can be labelled as clueless.

As a leader, keep in mind that you need to put people in the right positions and you will lose talent if you don't manage personalities and positions properly. Always keep an individual's personality type in mind when making assignments.

I can remember a team where, to be fair, they rotated the duty of recording the meeting minutes among the team members. Sounds great. However, when I took minutes, the results could only be described as thin, as I was always participating and engaged in the meeting. In short order I was relieved of that duty, and that was very much the right decision.

Over the next four chapters, we will examine the four classic personality types while identifying both the positive and negative attributes attached to each.

Under each personality profile, I have included some alignments with other common personality programs , as well as my own examples from popular culture like the characters from *Seinfeld*,[65] *The Office*,[66] and *Peanuts*[67] (the TV shows and cartoon strip).

Energy (introvert/extrovert) and focus (people/process) are the criteria we will use to establish our personality profiles.

If we chart these criteria, four distinct types are revealed. These four types are considered major types, so they are often referred to as the four common types of people in the world. As we shall see, most individuals fit comfortably into at least one of these four types.

Figure 15. Personality Profile Grid

	Extroverted	**Introverted**
Process	**Driver** (extrovert, process)	**Thinker** (introvert, process)
People	**Expressive** (extrovert, people)	**Amiable** (introvert, people)

PART 3

KEY LESSON

If we examine an individual's personality through the criteria of energy and focus, it demonstrates, with these criteria anyway, there are only four types of people in the world. While there is some variance within that profile, almost everyone can be captured under one of the four types.

Where you get your energy will dictate if you are introverted or extraverted, and where you place your focus will determine if you are project-focused or people-focused.

Each of these four personality types will display a consistent behaviour over time and that predictability will help you understand your talent.

CHAPTER 15

*You can knock me down
but I get up twice as strong.
—Lewis Hamilton*

CHAPTER 15

The Drivers

Drivers are confident, dominant, and no-nonsense. They are in charge and in control, and usually deliver the required results on time and on budget. They get it done (whatever "it" is). Drivers tend to be in leadership roles a bit more than the other three personality types by about ten per cent.

Drivers are focused, goal-oriented, and typically seen working in high-stress situations.

At the extremes, Drivers can be demanding workaholics—often sharp and belittling to staff.

Positive Driver Attributes

Action/task-oriented	Direct	Assertive
Dynamic	Self-driven	Competitive
Decisive	Goal-oriented	Determined
Confident	Tenacious	Fast paced
Entrepreneurial	Ambitious	Independent
Delegator	Multitasker	Strong Administrator

Negative Driver Attributes

Competitive   Insensitive   Domineering
Stubborn   Impatient/high stress   Emotional
"Short Fuse"   Intolerant   Abrupt
                    No/little Collaboration

Figure 16. Typical Driver Profiles

According to this personality system	You are a...
4-animal system	Lion
4-bird system	Eagle
On the DISC profile	D–Direct/controlling
Colours (insights)	Blue
Enneagram	Adventurer/achiever
PSI	Controller
Fisher Temperament Inventory	Testosterone
Stereotypical job	Elite level athlete, Olympian
***Peanuts* character**	Lucy Bit of a bully, very assertive, self-centred, even vain.
***Seinfeld* character**	Jerry Seinfeld Clear leader of the group. The only one who accomplishes anything and often the only one with a job. Must always win.
***The Office* character**	Jim Halpert Though not always obvious, Jim was always looking to win at sales, at least against Dwight. Literally stole the girl of his dreams (Pam) from Roy.
Well-known Driver	Donald Trump

PART 3

> *I think if you don't touch the wall in Monaco,*
> *You're not on the limit.*[68]
> *–Lance Stroll, Canadian racing driver*

Working for Drivers

A Driver's focus is always on the process for the projects, so when working for a Driver, always be ready to discuss the status of things (and never say, "I don't know." Saying, "I will find out" is a much better response to a Driver).

Drivers give their thoughts and direction in a short-and-sweet manner and expect the reports back to them to be the same, so make sure you are focused to deliver in that manner.

Although Drivers love to test you, most of their problem solving and decision making is done in isolation. Unfortunately, often this turns out to be a rushed decision.

Further limiting these rush decisions for Drivers is their poor listening skills and a brash outspokenness. Ensure they are properly briefed on the projects and be ready for pointed questions.

> *If you are in control,*
> *You're not going fast enough.*[69]
> *–Parnelli Jones, racing driver*

When you are given the opportunity to participate, shy away from a single recommendation (that can be discounted out of hand) and put the focus on developing options with clear parameters that they can readily consider and evaluate. Be task-focused by providing a problem–solution orientation.

Let the Driver decide, but don't hesitate to generate clear alternatives.

Drivers are protective of their schedule and value the economy of their time. Be efficient and precise and shy away from small talk and personal discussions. Be on time.

FOCUS THE TEAM

Drivers have little-to-no empathy for others, so personality conflicts can often start with a Driver's insensitive words or the harsh handling of a team member.

> *Winning is everything.*
> *The only ones who remember you when*
> *you come second are your wife and your dog.*[70]
> *–Damon Hill*

If a Driver Works for You

Having a strong Driver is a bit like having a thoroughbred and trying to keep the horse on the track. With the right motivation, they can be a massive asset; just be ready to be throw once and a while. Ambition is an important thing for Drivers, so know this: they are already thinking about taking over your job.

The best way to motivate a Driver is to provide them the freedom and independence to control their own projects. They love to be in control and run their own show. Challenging opportunities of an urgent nature are something they strive for. Do not overplay the odds because they will have already thought it through and will only chase favourable risk-reward situations.

As the leader of a Driver, it is critical where you place that individual in a team environment. Here are three things to consider with a Driver (remember we are examining the extreme of the type).

- Control issues: Drivers can be aggressive and overbearing, so you need to be clear about boundaries and responsibilities (specifically, where theirs end).

- Outspokenness: Drivers can be abrupt and often do not suffer fools lightly. As a result, their treatment of staff can be harsh and intimidating. They can be overly critical—even aggressive—in their opinions.

- Poor Listening Skills: To ensure your key messages get through, deliver in different mediums and follow up when face to face (e.g., "Did you get my email about production?").

CHAPTER 16

*The most amiable people are those who
least wound the self love of others.
–Jean de La Bruyère*

CHAPTER 16

The Amiables

Amiables are relationship-focused and incredibly supportive of others. They seek respect and appreciation and are the stabilizing force on the team. Often seen as the diplomats, Amiables are the "glue" that holds the group together. Amiables are experts in bringing people together. They want harmony and will work hard to keep everyone happy.

At the extreme, they can shut down and hold back their opinions, especially if their values are challenged or compromised.

Positive Amiable Attributes

Feeler	Fair	Listener
Introverted	Calm	Sensitive
Consensus builder	Trusting	Staff focused
Casual	Caring	Patient
Low-key	Considerate	Kind
Sympathetic	Approachable	Dependable/methodical

Negative Amiable Attributes

Less assertive
Holds back opinion
Risk Adverse

Slow and methodical
Easily used by others
Easily hurt by others
Puts own needs last

Too accommodating
Resistant to change
Averse to confrontation

Figure 17. Typical Amiable Profiles

According to this personality system	You are a...
4-animal system	Otter
4-bird system	Dove
On the DISC profile	S–Indirect/supporting
Colours (insights)	Orange
Enneagram	Peacekeeper/observer
PSI	Supporter
Fisher Temperament Inventory	Estrogen
Stereotypical job	HR/guidance counsellor, life coach
Peanuts **character**	Charlie Brown Very naïve and just wants to have a good relationship with everyone. Believes in people yet often taken advantage of.
Seinfeld **character**	Elaine Benes Forever seeking harmony with the group. No secret was ever truly in the vault
The Office **character**	Pam Beesly Always puts others' needs ahead of herself—even those of Michael Scott
Well-known Amiable	Mother Teresa

PART 3

We meet so many people in life,
but we connect to the heart of very few.[71]
–Avijeet Das, Indian poet and author

If You Work for an Amiable

The Amiables' focus is on the people involved in the project, and they put relationships first.

If you work for an Amiable, it is critical to establish a solid relationship and do not attempt to rush it. Put the work to one side and focus on building trust. Try to grow that trust over time with the goal of becoming one of the "insiders," or trusted advisors.

Amiables like to gather the opinions of everyone. Time is not a concern, but the thoroughness of the opinions surveyed usually is.

> *Truth is everybody is going to hurt you:*
> *you just gotta find the ones worth suffering for.*[72]
> *–Bob Marley*

If an Amiable Works for You

Amiables grow through collaboration with people, so be patient with the stories about people's experiences and life lessons.

Amiables appreciate the stability of a routine and calm environment. They do not manage change well and will inevitably support the low-risk options.

Trust is extremely important to Amiables, and if a decision or change in direction violates that trust, they may just passively comply, but in reality, are checking out.

Because of this, ensure any changes are discussed well in advance with the Amiables on the team. You want them to be ambassadors of the project and they are an important communication conduit.

CHAPTER 17

*I am an extremely strong extrovert
but I'm not that into people.
I just like to hang around people.
–Joseph P. Connelly*

CHAPTER 17

The Expressives

The underlying motivation for Expressives is to be liked, so they are usually seeking approval. Thus, they like to talk... a lot... usually about themselves.

Naturally charismatic, they use their quick wit and sincere approach to win you over. Often emotional, they are easy to read and often wear their heart on their sleeve.

Positive Expressive Attributes

Energetic	Likeable	Excitable
Motivating	Creative	Spontaneous
Easygoing	Direct	Fun/funny
Ambitious	Self Confident	Enthusiastic
Talkative	Intuitive	Friendly
Persuasive	Charismatic	Motivator

THE EXPRESSIVES

Negative Expressive Attributes

Impatient and easily bored
Cocky, even arrogant
Prone to sweeping generalizations
Unrealistic
Whimsical
Impulsive
Undisciplined
Short attention span
Prone to exaggeration
Self-indulgent

Figure 18. Typical Expressive Profiles

According to this personality system	You are a...
4-animal system	Golden Labrador/any dog really
4-bird system	Peacock/parrot
On the DISC profile	I –Directing/supporting
Colours (insights)	Green
Enneagram	Helper/romantic
PSI	Promoter
Fisher Temperament Inventory	Dopamine
Stereotypical job	Actor/motivational speaker/politician
Peanuts character	Snoopy The whimsical outlier who would resist much and obey little. Dances like nobody is watching and does not care what others think.
Seinfeld character	Cosmo Kramer Just the hair tells you everything. Impulsive, rebellious, creative to the point of off-the-wall, carefree.
The Office character	Michael G. Scott Larger than life with limited attention to detail
Well-known Expressive	Drake (at a basketball game during playoffs!)

> *I don't know how much more expressive
> you can get than being a rock and roll singer.*[73]
> *–Robert Plant, lead singer, Led Zeppelin*

If You Work for an Expressive

If you find yourself working for an Expressive, the best thing you can do is "get on the bus" with them and subscribe to their vision and future orientation.

Expressives like to spend time working with others; if you work for one, you may find yourself managing their energy. As Expressives like to provide story after story, you may find yourself having to say, "I'm sorry, but I must go now and do good elsewhere."

When making decisions, present testimonials and anecdotes to support the recommendations because the opinion of others is important to Expressives.

Expressive are often disorganized, even scrambled, so help them get organized and stay on track. They often hate dealing with details, so taking that over is of considerable value to them.

> *There are two things people want
> more than sex and money...
> recognition and praise.*[74]
> *–Mary Kay Ash, American businesswoman*

If an Expressive Works for You

Expressives like to be the centre of attention, so public recognition and awards are strong motivators. Expressives like to promote success and the idea that they are winning, so there is a usually a conspicuous display of the latest styles and trends.

FOCUS THE TEAM

Expressives can easily bite off more than they can chew because of their unwavering confidence. This can lead to problems with procrastination and even an inability to finish. This book is a fitting example of this issue, as it took me four years to research and produce, with a few stops and starts along the way (but I digress).

At the extreme, Expressives can be major discipline problems. They are verbally talented, think quickly on their feet, and are excellent at logical arguments, all of which are challenging for the other types. Expressives tend to be natural leaders, so they don't just quit; they tend to quit and lead all the other staff to walk out with them.

PART 3

CHAPTER 18

Thinking: The talking of the soul with itself.
—Plato

CHAPTER 18

The Thinkers

The Thinkers are all about facts and data, with a heavy reliance on rules and processes. Often deep in thought, they rarely share nor care about your or anyone else's feelings.

Thinkers are quiet, cautious, methodical, and unerringly logical. They love to follow rules and protocols and are usually meticulously prepared with facts and data. Thinkers take pride in controlling themselves, but they are especially fond of controlling others.

Positive Thinker Attributes

Rule follower	Emotionally controlled	Orderly
Systematic	Neat/tidy	Accurate
Valuer of routine	Process-driven	Serious
Thorough	Organized	Deliberate
Detail-oriented	Methodical	Perfectionist
Dependable	Task-focused	Analytical

Negative Thinker Attributes

Resistant to change
Rigid on rules
Workaholic

Stubborn
Antisocial
Lack of emotion
Skeptical

Risk adverse
Worried/stressed
Critical of others' behaviours

Figure 19. Typical Thinker Profiles

According to this personality system	You are a...
4-animal system	Beaver
4-bird system	Owl
On the DISC profile	C–Indirect/controlling
Colours (insights)	Gold
Enneagram	Asserter/perfectionist
PSI	Analyst
Fisher Temperament Inventory	Serotonin
Stereotypical job	Tax auditor/accountant
***Peanuts* character**	Linus Quiet, always thinking, self reflective, skeptical, worries a lot.
***Seinfeld* character**	George Costanza More extreme than Linus, paranoid, antisocial, exaggerates risks, always scheming.
***The Office* character**	Dwight Schrute Similar to George Costanza, paranoid and antisocial, only in an XL size
Well-known Thinker	Albert Einstein

*First doubt, then inquire, then discover.
This has been the process with all great thinkers.*[75]
–Henry Thomas Buckle, English historian

If You Work for a Thinker

If you work for a Thinker, know your stuff and expect more questions than usual. Back up everything with data, studies, instructions, examples, and any other information available. Thinkers tend to be information junkies with voracious appetites for all types of reports. Thinkers demand much of themselves and others, so be organized with clear and detailed responses.

Do not waste time with small talk and opinions. They do not care. Be patient with decisions because Thinkers would rather let deadlines pass than be rushed into a decision.

*Every deep thinker is more afraid of being understood
than of being misunderstood.* [76]
–Friedrich Nietzsche

If a Thinker Works for You

Thinkers prefer to demonstrate their competence by working independently, so give them opportunities to showcase their intelligence and problem solving. Note that Thinkers can be very inflexible in applying rules with others, and this can cause friction.

FOCUS THE TEAM

PART 4

Be The Leader

*I am on the side of good in you
and I hope it manifests itself.
–Jordan Peterson, interview
with Dr. Mattias Desmet*

CHAPTER 19

Leading The Team

*Morale in an organization does not mean
that people get along together.
The test is performance, not conformance.*[77]
–Peter Drucker, management expert

I can remember I had this small but talented team in the education field, and one day I noticed the junior member seemed very despondent, so I called her into my office for a chat.

She related to me that she did not feel a part of the team because she was the junior member and felt (incorrectly) that her clerical role was lacking in value. I had to admit, she had a pretty tough job answering inquiries, dealing with daily changes, and providing considerable student support. The irony was that she was great on the phone, with zero complaints in four years and a really positive team member, so this recent development was concerning.

I explained to her that she was exceptional at her job and a very important member of the team, but that sounded like rhetoric, so I went further.

I asked her to consider what would happen if her performance began to slip. Because we had a small team, such declines would demand another on the team step in and help. With fewer staff working on all the right stuff, the overall department results would suffer. It would create a bit of a domino effect. Instead of moving forward, we would just be treading water, neither moving forward nor back—and over time slowly sinking.

In fact, just someone taking a day off meant that there would be no course development that day due to job covers.

We spoke for thirty minutes about all the good she contributed, and when she left my office, she understood that just because she was junior in position, which did not mean she was not a valuable team member. She WAS important but just didn't realize it.

As a leader, you need to read the mood and stay on top of the energy.

Leadership is not easy. It is long hours, complex decisions, and few friends. It does, however, get easier when you know your personality type and the leadership style you usually engage.

In the story above, the staff member was clearly an Amiable, so I put on my Amiable hat and mostly listened.

When I spoke, it was usually to clarify. We took our time and had a great exchange. In the end, she understood her value much better.

That day was a win, but some days the sun does not shine like it should. Some days the personalities clash.

For a long time, I believed that the Amiables were the most valuable of all the personality types because they kept the other three from killing each other. Conflict happens in the best of teams, families, and relationships, and most of it is healthy. While Amiables provide the social connectivity, they also serve as a social buffer between the other types, who have natural conflict points.

For our leadership purposes here, we will look at three areas of potential conflict and how each personality would react. Specifically, we will examine their communication style, time management, and approach to decision making.

PART 4

As we have demonstrated, your job as leader is to get results, so how you manage these personalities is critical to achieving your goals. Do not waste the energy of the team on interpersonal conflict and other non-productive activities. Address conflict immediately before it becomes a problem.

As we shall see, a lot of the conflict emerges between Drivers and Amiables, and between Expressives and Thinkers. They just rub each other the wrong way.

I will again utilize the extremes of each type to showcase that particular behaviour.

Communication Styles

The single biggest problem in communication is the illusion that it has taken place.[78]
–George Bernard Shaw

Figure 20. How Each Personality Type Communicates

DRIVERS (blunt)	**AMIABLES (soft)**
"Short and sweet" (to the point) Direct, blunt, quick	Soft, slow, and methodical Sensitive, cautious, paced, and staged
EXPRESSIVES (quick)	**THINKERS (details)**
Big-picture summary Few details	Every detail possible Every possible angle

Drivers and Amiables

As you can see from the communication chart, Drivers are blunt and to the point, while Amiables will be more paced and cautious. Amiables may even release just a bit of information and then judge the reactions, while Drivers are much more likely to just put it out there, on the table all at once.

Drivers often shoot from the hip, while Amiables are measured and cautious. It is easy to imagine a scenario where the Amiable is completely overpowered by the Driver on how best to communicate.

Specifically, Drivers are usually best at dealing with external communications, such as the hard question tossed out by media.

Amiables are well skilled for internal communication, particularly when delivering sad news. Their soft, calm, and genuine manner is well suited for communications within the organization.

Expressives and Thinkers

When I look at the Expressives, I could best describe their communication style as incomplete (I am an extreme Expressive, so I can be brutally honest here). Expressives are great at giving big-picture summaries, unencumbered by any solid plans or details.

In contrast to this, the Thinkers take extraordinary pride in delivering every minute detail and fact available. For Thinkers, the more information, the better, and they get frustrated when they are not allowed to cover everything, whether relevant or not.

In fact, the ongoing conflict that exists in many organizations between accounting and sales is grounded in the fundamental differences in the personality styles of each department. Most people in accounting are Thinkers, where those in sales tend to be Expressives. As a result, accounting generally wants all the details communicated immediately and sales is more about, "I will get it to you when I find some time (thus, not perceived a priority)."

Time Management

The more sand has escaped from the hourglass of our life, the clearer we should see through it.[79]
–Machiavelli

Figure 21. How Each Personality Type Manages Time

DRIVERS (Guarded) Protected schedule Often alone/with one other	**AMIABLES (Open)** Open-door policy Interact with many
EXPRESSIVES (Spontaneous) Prefers group Limelight with team (feedback)	**THINKERS (Controlled)** Controlled Alone (studying reports)

Drivers and Amiables

Drivers jealously guard their time by protecting their schedule and insulating themselves, while Amiables have an open-door policy that tries to deal with issues immediately. Drivers will spend much of their time alone or in discussions with a one or two trusted advisors. Even at that, meetings with the Driver in these circumstances are brief and direct. Conflict arises when the Amiable wants to engage everyone to make the decision while the Driver just wants to decide and move on.

Amiables like to connect people with people but Drivers, not so much.

Expressives and Thinkers

Expressives love to be spontaneous and are always ready to have a quick meeting to discuss the issue (and any other topics, for that matter). If it involves the opportunity for the Expressive to be in the limelight and present the idea, then the meeting will be sooner rather than later.

Like Drivers, Thinkers also jealously guard their time, only more so. They also like to be alone, so they can read relevant material thoroughly. This makes them appear cold, but they are just more comfortable being alone with their own thoughts.

Thinkers have very structured schedules, while Expressives tend to run by how the day is going. Expressives think nothing of changing or cancelling plans at a moment's notice, and this never sits well with the highly scheduled Thinkers.

Approach to Decision Making

It is in your moments of decision that your destiny is shaped.[80]
–Tony Robbins, motivational speaker

Figure 22. How Each Personality Type Makes Decisions

DRIVERS (quick and solo)	AMIABLES (Slow with many)
Quick	Slow, methodical, thorough
Solo/single expert	Collaboration and feedback
Single authority	Everyone votes
EXPRESSIVES (Spontaneous)	**THINKERS (Methodical)**
Creative collaborator	Singular (no one better/smarter)
Spontaneous	Methodical
Exaggerator of potential	Exaggerator of risk

Drivers and Amiables

Surprisingly, Drivers can make the wrong decision for three main reasons.

Drivers will focus on the short-term symptoms of a problem and not the problem itself. Drivers like to make quick decisions because they don't like problems hanging around. In addition, Drivers often make the decision alone or with a close confidante. These three factors contribute to Drivers arriving at the wrong solution.

Amiables, by contrast, will want time to survey everyone for their opinion and investigate workable solutions (time conflict). This can be seen to dilute their authority, but that approach is low risk because it distributes the decision making (authority conflict). Time is of no consequence, and an Amiable would begin by designing a plan to gather the feedback. They may even collect input on that plan - the plan to gather input! (process conflict).

Drivers have no problem making the decision but the Amiables always want to put it to a vote.

Expressives and Thinkers

Expressives assemble their brightest and best people for a quick collaboration and decision. Thinkers would be aghast at this approach because they really do believe there is no one better qualified than themselves. They often discount the opinions of others because the only things that matter are facts. They decide in isolation but will be methodical in their steps at arriving at a decision just in case anyone challenges them on it.

In this chapter, I have tried to provide some insights into the common points of conflict between the four personalities. Of course, real-world applications are not simple and personalities are far more complex than these two criteria of energy and focus.

My intent here is to help you see the conflict coming and react accordingly. If you do not see the bus coming, then it is more likely you are going to get flattened by it.

PART 4

CHAPTER 20

*Change means movement, movement means friction,
only in the frictionless vacuum of
a nonexistent abstract world
can movement or change occur without that
abrasive friction of conflict.*
–Saul Alinsky, American community activist and writer

CHAPTER 20

Keeping the Trust

As you can see from the previous chapter, conflict can arise easily and between different personalities almost naturally. It is your job as leader to ensure you put the right people in the right roles in the first place. The benefits of knowing the personality preferences of the team members are vital when assigning responsibilities. For example, do not put Expressives in charge of detailed tasks. They will lose interest almost immediately.

It always amazed me why managers assigned responsibilities to individuals who hated those assignments, based on their personality profiles. Leaders know to play to the strengths of the team, not the weaknesses. This would be like, in sports, asking your top goal scorer to play defensively.

When I speak of trust, recognize that it is built slowly, sometimes over years, but it is lost in moments. In times of change (which is all the time), personality conflicts arise more readily because most individuals dislike change. Change creates stress, and one of the greatest stressors is a leadership change. Even though all indications may be that it is only the leader changing, everyone under the leader feels vulnerable right to the front lines. On several occasions, I have seen a leadership change brought down from a higher authority that has decimated an organization for several years because the moves were never fully thought out, the message seemed hastily assembled and questionable in logic, and the communication delivery absurd. The organization lost its focus and the energy was disrupted.

Once, in one of theses management shakeups, the board explained to the staff that the reason for the unexpected departures was a "new direction." When one of the staff (from my team, of course) asked what exactly the new direction was, they stumbled and did not have an answer. As a result, the board was caught and lost all trust with the staff. More departures ensued.

> *The glory built upon a lie soon becomes*
> *a most unpleasant encumbrance.*[81]
> *–Mark Twain*

Another great destroyer of trust is the corporate reorganization. In typical reorganizations, the teams are reset, but the trust is tested. The productivity plummets because everyone changes their focus to assessing their own future (should I stay or should I go?).

My friend in tourism, Julie Canning, used to be fond of saying, "You can't jump rope when you are gazing at your navel." This is a brilliant saying because you cannot be committed to your job (jumping rope) when you are looking at your future and considering your options (gazing at your navel).

In reorganizations, individuals with strong interpersonal skills move on while the mediocre ones stay. This makes sense because those who are confident in their talents are also confident in their ability to get another position elsewhere.

Those who stay are inevitably given more workload—at least in the short term—but rarely more responsibility. The culture tanks. Notice how once the energy and focus are affected, it leads to more frustration and more departures, further weakening the talent pool.

PART 4

RESULTS MATTER

*A team is not a group of people
that work together,
a team is a group of people that
trust each other.*[82]
–Simon Sinek, author

Absence of trust is recognized as the first stage in a team's decline in Patrick Lencioni's excellent book, *Five Dysfunctions of a Team: A Leadership Fable*.[83] I highly recommend this work when tasked with turning your team around.

The next stages identified by Lencioni include fear of conflict (lack of risk-taking), lack of commitment (absence of effort), avoidance of accountability (not my job), and inattention to results (lack of consequences). I have identified these here because I find it remarkable that once trust is lost, the other four stages appear with surprising speed. If you find yourself in a low-trust situation, be aware of the other behaviours that will, if unchecked, surely arise.

Figure 23. Five Dysfunctions of a Team

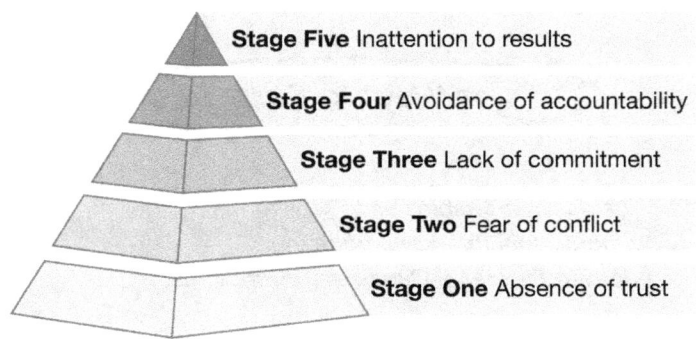

Note: from Patrick Lencioni's Five Dysfunctions of a Team: A Leadership Fable

KEEPING TRUST

Trust is really made up of two components: integrity and capability. Integrity is usually covered by two questions, are they fair and do they care?

Fair—Do they apply the rules equally?

Care—Are they open, honest, and balanced?

Capability is the ability to demonstrate they have the education, skills, and experience for that position, but capabilities go a bit further, in that trust can be reinforced with a history of success. A formidable reputation will add to your credibility.

Figure 24. Components of Trust

TRUST = INTEGRITY and CAPABILITY

INTEGRITY	CAPABILITIES
Are they fair and do they care?	Are they competent?

Three Ways to Build Trust

Trust is what enables us to look at each other without running away screaming.[84]
—Jordan Peterson, Canadian psychologist

1. Consistently tell the truth

Even the perception of a lie will cause trust to slip quickly, so deal with the truth by delivering it first. If you can't talk about it, say so.

2. Deliver on your promises

PART 4

Only make promises you are one hundred per cent sure you can deliver. There is nothing wrong with being upfront and clear on what you can and cannot deliver.

3. Own your mistakes

Everyone makes mistakes and stepping up and taking responsibility for those mistakes will build trust within the team. Nothing kills trust faster than blaming another for one's misstep.

Regardless of the level of trust with your team, I have always found value in encouraging participation in ongoing education with the subtle goal of getting the team to rally around something. I have used many management books throughout the years for this rallying point, but James P. Owen's focus on integrity in *Cowboy Ethics* is well worth mentioning.[85]

I keep a copy of his "Code of the West" in my wallet on a business card. With sayings like "Talk less and say more" and "Remember some things aren't for sale," *Cowboy Ethics* is a terrific book to rally your people around. Take a chapter a week and spend ten minutes talking about it in your next meeting. Start with what they liked and what they didn't and then let them pick the next book.

By endorsing education, you create an atmosphere of continuous improvement. This pushes not only the team to be better, but also the individuals on the team. I always urged my team to take something, anything, they were interested in, so they never stopped learning. I was never that concerned about what they took, as long as they took something and grew intellectually.

If you as a leader are committed to making the individuals on the team better, the trust will build.

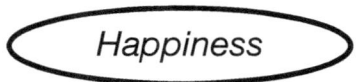

Very little is needed to make a happy life.
It is all within yourself, in your way of thinking.[86]
–Marcus Aurelius

BE THE LEADER

Please allow me to close this chapter with some thoughts about happiness.

You can only achieve real happiness by understanding yourself and knowing what makes you happy. This is another important reason to know yourself.

As we have seen from the personality profiles, we are all different, with different values and motivations. Never stop learning about yourself and your own personality. The more you understand yourself, the easier you will find it to understand others.

Throughout my career, I have encountered many people who were miserable because they were in a job that was counter to their personality. I understand this is a problem, with about seventy-five per cent of the labour force not happy in their present position. If you know what makes you happy, you can take the steps to move your career to a happier place.

Happiness varies from person to person, but it is connected to purpose (Why are we here?), engagement with others (positive social interaction), and harmony (respect for team, managing setbacks, and emotional control).

The Myers Briggs Type Indicator (MBTI) platform (psychometrics.com) is a great place for personality information and they have just completed a large and comprehensive study on happiness. The research found that happiness comprises three elements.[87]

Figure 25. Components of Happiness (MBTI)

REWARD	**SELF**	**SOCIAL**
• Financial	• Creative Expression	Positive interaction with others
• Prestige	• Ownership	
• Security	• Individuality	
• Promotion		

PART 4

1. Extrinsic rewards: financial, prestige, security, and promotion

I have heard it said it is not that financial reward is the only motivation, but it is so far ahead of the rest, it makes the others seem insignificant. This may be true; however, I believe it depends more on your personality and stage in life.

2. Self expression: owning process, creativity, and individuality

The actual accomplishment of your results, especially when unique to you, can be satisfying to many ("I did that," but also, "I did it my way").

3. Positive social interaction with others

There is considerable happiness in experiencing achievements with your work colleagues. Just look at any championship sports team and the camaraderie that can lead to lifelong friendships.

Remember these factors when thinking about your own team and their level of happiness.

CHAPTER 21

One of the greatest mistakes is to judge policies and programs by their intentions rather than their results.
–Milton Friedman, American economist

CHAPTER 21

Final Words

I began this leadership project by trying to answer the fundamental question of what actually makes a great leader. I reviewed about a hundred attributes, but in the end, leadership is not about attributes.

Leadership is about results.

Certainly, in some environments, the right attributes can help results, but they do not necessarily guarantee them. So why do we focus incessantly on changing the leader and not on improving the process? For this reason, this book took the position of focusing on results and how to get better at producing them.

Better results really will give us better leaders.

The Results Matter approach gives you better results, so you can become a better leader. The more you use the matrix, the more comfortable you and your team will become with it, and I truly hope you find it valuable in all applications.

*Now this is not the end,
it is not even the beginning of the end.
But it is, perhaps, the end of the beginning.
–Winston Churchill*

EPILOGUE

My brilliant mother passed away at age ninety-nine, but I was extremely happy that my sons saw her just a few months before.

She had lived for many years alone in the tall adult apartments by Yonge Street in Toronto. I recall that when my boys were little, they loved to watch the heavy traffic on Highway 401 from her twelfth-floor balcony.

We went to see her one afternoon for high tea. Even at ninety-nine, she was still bright, alert, and very engaging. She was known to the other grandchildren as "Wiki Grandma."

As we visited that day, I smiled as I noticed how she subtly tested the boys about their knowledge in many fields, like she often did with me when I was younger. She always had the best questions, and everyone misses her wisdom.

Returning to the car after tea, my youngest son (at age twenty-eight) commented, "You know Dad—she really is the smartest person I know."

My mother provided great input and continuous motivation for this book. She supported the contention that results really do matter.

In her case, she achieved her goal of a university education for each of her boys, as all four eventually graduated (admittedly, some faster than others). My older brothers went on to be a lawyer, a dentist, and a teacher. I went into business and have been grateful for several exciting and successful careers, including political office.

This book is dedicated to her memory and her never-ending support of everything I ever tried.

Appendix

Onboarding Checklist

Introduce the new employee to the organization and orient them to the company's culture.

Orientation

- ☑ Education on the company's history
- ☑ Company's competitive positioning
- ☑ Company's marketing strategies
- ☑ Company's approach to market
- ☑ Common HR norms (holidays to lunchroom)
- ☑ Common attire, company clothing, premium clothing
- ☑ Company calendar
- ☑ Early schedule—day one
- ☑ Early schedule—day two
- ☑ Early schedule—day three
- ☑ Welcome function, emails, lunch, reception (depending on position)
- ☑ Policies and procedures (first aid, safety, emergency)
- ☑ Employee handbook review (if available)
- ☑ Housekeeping (HR paperwork, payroll, deductions, benefits, government paperwork)

Expectations

- ☑ 30-day goals confirmed
- ☑ 60-day goals confirmed
- ☑ 90-day goals confirmed
- ☑ Key performance indicators established
- ☑ Company values presented
- ☑ Company culture explained

Accreditation

- ☑ Access to company's financial assets
  (Credit cards, bank drafts, etc.)
- ☑ Signing authority
  (Bank signature, limit amount)
- ☑ Access to company electronically
  (Network, intranet, Wi-Fi, home technology)
- ☑ Access to company's electronic assets
  (Cell, laptop, printer, etc.)
- ☑ Access to the company HQ
  (Parking, building access, supplies, warehouse)

Copyright, 2020: Results Matter (division of Straight Shooters Marketing)

Acknowledgements

*If I have seen further than others,
it is by standing upon
the shoulders of giants.*[88]
–Isaac Newton

Many thanks to the following individuals who have contributed to making me a better leader. Without your advice and support, this project would not have been possible.

Elizabeth Connelly

Lacy Leiffers	John Kozole	Erwin Bartell
Glenn Street	Riley Miller	Corinne Wilkinson
Camille Sojer	Jim Fitzowich	Roger Jewett
Lou Schizas	Kevin Yates	Jaime Miller
Jack Connelly	Brett Albers	Shea Connelly

*The object of life is not to be on the
side of the majority but to escape,
finding oneself in the ranks of the insane.*[89]
–Marcus Aurelius

About the Author

*A great fire burns within me,
but no one stops to warm themselves at it,
and passers-by only see a wisp of smoke.*[90]
–Van Gogh

Joseph Connelly likes to speak of his unique business experiences as a "career of many colours." He has a broad history of executive experience in diverse industries, including tourism, online education, finance, software development, and digital outdoor media. Joseph would be the first to admit to a brilliant career due to his many excellent mentors and the great advice provided by these leaders.

Throughout his career, Joseph has sought to answer a question that has puzzled scholars for centuries, namely, what makes a great leader?

To that end, he spent four years taking courses, researching leadership offerings and interviewing entrepreneurs and leaders in blue-chip corporations, not-for-profits, and small and medium enterprises. Even a few well known politicians were asked that seminal question, what makes a great leader?

His findings suggest that while you may not be able to teach leadership, you can certainly teach leaders to achieve better results. The answers to his six questions establish an accountability matrix that will unite and focus your team to drive better results.

Better results for better leaders.

Joseph can be reached for comment, consultation and speaking engagements at Joseph@resultsmatter.app.

End Notes

1. David Bromwich, The Intellectual Life of Edmund Burke (Harvard University Press, 2014).
2. David Bromwich, The Intellectual Life of Edmund Burke (Harvard University Press, 2014).
3. Richard Burke, The Political Life of Edmund Burke (Princeton University Press, 2017).
4. Bill Owens, American Politician, Brainy Quote 167728 (Brainyquote.com).
5. Online article, Medium.com, The 25 Greatest Leaders of All Time.

    Online article, weareteachers.com, Forty Famous World Leaders Your Students Should Know, 2022.

    Online article, thetoptens.com, Top Ten Most Important Leaders in World History, 2002.

    Online article, thetoptens.com, Most Influential Leaders of the 20th Century, 2002.

    Online Article, Industryleadersmagazine.com, Patrick Alain, Leadership and Ten Great Leaders from History, 2012.
6. Winston Churchill, The Second World War: Alone, (Audio Go, MP3 Book) 2008.
7. Pablo Picasso, Spanish Painter, Brainy Quote 120309 (Brainyquote.com).

8. Scott Adams, American Writer/Cartoonist, Good Reads 1116406 (goodreads.com).

9. Bernie Sanders, American Politician, Quote Citation (Quote-citation.com).

10. Freddie Gray, The Death of Political Authority (The Spectator Magazine) 2022.

11. Victor Davis Hanson, A Cabinency of Dunces (Las Vegas Review) 2022.

12. ACT Research, American College Test Grad Class Database (Act.org) 2022.

13. General Social Survey on Mean IQ, NORC - National Opinion Research Center (University of Chicago) 1960 to 2010.

14. Online Article, Peter Dockrill, IQ Scores are Falling in 'Worrying" Reversal of Intelligence Boom (Sciencealert.com) 2018.

15. Online Quote, Dylan Machan, They Say So (Theysaidso.com).

16. Online Article, Gabriela Hammond, Statue of Liberty Meaning: What She Stands For (Statueoflibertytour.com)

17. Online Article, Symbolism of the Statue of Liberty (Wondersoftheworld.net).

18. Online Article, Secret Places, European Immigrant Cheered Lady Liberty (Ragingnelliebly.com) 2002.

19. Online Quote, Peter Mere Latham, They Said So (Theysaidso.com).

20. Joseph P Connelly, Results Matter Seminar, University of Calgary, 2019.

21. Online Quote, Simon Sinek, Starter Story (starterstory.com).

22. Online Article, Joseph Folkman, To Get Results, the Best Leaders Push and Pull Their Teams (Harvard Business Review) 2022.

23. Peter Drucker, The Essential Drucker (Regan Books) 2003

24. E.W. Palmer - speech at the 1946 International Rotary Convention, Kingsport, Tennessee.

25. Online Quote, John Kotter, 5 Inspiring Change Leadership Quotes (Ciotalknetwork.com).

26. Online Article, Peter Economy, Seven Keys to Becoming a Remarkably Effective Leader (Inc Magazine) 2016.

27. Online Article, Geoff Loftus, Four Keys to Great Leadership (Forbes Magazine) 2012.
28. Online Article, Carole Vallone Mitchell, Three Keys to Influential Leadership (Fast Company Magazine) 2015.
29. Online Article, Riz Pasha, 117 Greatest Peter Drucker Quotes of All Time (successfeed.com) 2018.
30. Online Article, Daniel Goleman, Leadership That Gets Results (Harvard Business Review) 2000.
31. Moldoveanu and Narayandas, The Future of Leadership Development, Chapter One, Educating the Next Generation (Harvard Business Review) 2019.
32. Moldoveanu and Narayandas, The Future of Leadership Development, Chapter One, Educating the Next Generation (Harvard Business Review) 2019.
33. John Kotter, Leading Change (Harvard University Press) 1996.
34. Kootz and O'Donnell, The Five Functions of Management (Management functions - Managementstudyguide.com).
35. Martin Luther King, Martin Luther Speaks (Audiobook by Intellect Inspire)
36. Gallop, The State of the American Workplace, Employee Engagement Insights for US Business Leaders, 2013
37. Carr, Reece, Kellerman, Robichaux, The Value of Belonging at Work (Harvard Business Review) 2019.
38. John Baldoni, Employee Engagement Does More Than Boost Productivity (Harvard Business Review) 2013.
39. Online Quote, Albert Einstein, Brainy Quote 148819 (Brainyquote.com).
40. Dean Kootz, Cold Fire (Hachette, UK) 2012.
41. Simon Sinek, Start with Why, How Great Leaders Inspire Everyone To Action (Amazon) 2011.
42. Morton Hanson, Great at Work – The Hidden Habits of Top Performers (Simon and Schuster) 2019.
43. James E Faust, Stories from My Life (Deseret Books) 2001.
44. Online Quote, Joe Namath, Quote Citation (Quote-citation.com).

45. Yogi Berra, The Yogi Book, I Really Didn't Say Everything I Said (Workman Publishing) 1998.
46. Needleman and Piazza, The Essential Marcus Aurelius (Tarcher Perigee) 2008.
47. Online Quote, George S. Patton, We Are the Mighty (Wearethemighty.com).
48. Online Quote, Harvey S. Firestone, Quote Citation (Quotecitation.com).
49. Online Article, Amanda Rutendo, Bruce Tuckman's Team Development Model (Academia.edu).
50. Online Article, Brandy Halladay, 2019 Hall of Fame Induction Speech, Cooperstown (Bluejaysnation.com).
51. Georg Joachim Rheticus, Austrian Astronomer, 1514-1574.
52. Online Article, Rotary International, The Four Way Test in a Post Truth Era (Rotary.org).
53. Online Quote, Albert Einstein, Relics World (Relicsworld.com).
54. Online Quote, Khlil Gibran, Brainy Quote (Brainyquote.com).
55. Online Article, How Fat is America? An Overview of Obesity Statistics (Livin3.com) 2022.
56. Online Article, Keith Ferrazzi, Technology Can Save Onboarding from Itself (Harvard Business Review) 2015.
57. Oxford Dictionary, 3rd Edition, "Onboarding" Definition.
58. Online Quote, Henry H. Neff, American Author, Quote Sayings (Quotesayings.net).
59. Nick Haslan, Bell Shaped Distribution of Personality Traits (SpringerLink) 2016.
60. Online Article, Madeline Ford, A History of Personality Psychology (Psychology.blog.motive.metrics.com).
61. Online Article, Myers and Briggs, 16 Personality Types (Truity.com).
62. Online Article, Fisher Temperament Inventory (test), (Psychmechanics.com)
63. Online Quote, General George S. Patton, American WWII General, (Storytick.com).

64. Online Article, Merrill and Reid, Social Styles Questionnaire (agilityportal.io) 2021
65. Online Article, Seinfeld (Seinfeldscripts.com).
66. Online Article, The Office (the-office-TV-show.com).
67. Online Article, Peanuts (peanuts.com).
68. Online Interview, Lawrence Edmonson, Lance Stroll Interview (ESPN.com).
69. Online Quote, Parnelli Jones (Theroadtripexpert.com).
70. Online Quote, Damon Hill (Theroadtripexpert.com).
71. Online Quote, Avijeet Das, Why the Silhouette? (Goodreaders.com).
72. Online Quote, Bob Marley, Good Reads 562872 (goodreads.com)
73. Online Quote, Robert Plant, Brainy Quote 472872 (Brianyquote.com)
74. Mary Kay Ash, Founder of May Key Cosmetics, Miracles Happen (Avon) 2003.
75. Online Quote, Henry Thomas Buckle (Wisefamousquotes.com).
76. Online Quote, Friedrich Nietzsche, Deep Thinking (Graciousquotes.com).
77. Online Quote, Peter Drucker (Quotenova.net).
78. Online Quote, George Bernard Shaw (Brainyquote.com).
79. Online Quote, Niccolò Machiavelli (Internetpoem.com).
80. Online Quote, Tony Robbins, Brainy Quote 147787 (Brainyquote.com).
81. Mark Alexander, The Timeless Wit and Wisdom of Mark Twain (Patriot Post).
82. Online Quote, Simon Sinek, Starter Story (Starterstory.com).
83. Patrick Lencioni, Five Dysfunctions of a Team, A Leadership Fable (Jossey-Bass) 2002.
84. Online Article, Jordan Peterson, Monday of Meaning, Oct. 31, 2022.
85. James P. Owen, Cowboy Ethics, What Wall Street Can Learn from the Code of the West (Stoecklein) 2005.
86. Needleman and Piazza, The Essential Marcus Aurelius (Tarcher Perigee) 2008.

87. Online Article, Shawn Bekker, What Makes People Happy at Work? (Psychometrics.com).

88. Online quote, Isaac Newton, Brainy Quote 135885 (Brainyquote.com).

89. Needleman and Piazza, The Essential Marcus Aurelius (Tarcher Perigee) 2008.

90. Online Quote, Vincent Van Gogh, Good Reads 188744 (goodreads.com).

www.ingramcontent.com/pod-product-compliance
Lightning Source LLC
Chambersburg PA
CBHW071921290426
44110CB00013B/1438